THAILAND

An Introduction to Modern Siam

The Asia Library

THAILAND: An Introduction to Modern Siam
by NOEL F. BUSCH

Additions to the Asia Library will be listed as they appear

THAILAND

An Introduction to Modern Siam

by

NOEL F. BUSCH

DRAWINGS BY ALAN THIELKER
MAP BY DOROTHY DE FONTAINE

D. VAN NOSTRAND COMPANY, Inc.
PRINCETON, NEW JERSEY
TORONTO   LONDON
NEW YORK

D. VAN NOSTRAND COMPANY, INC.

120 Alexander St., Princeton, New Jersey (*Principal office*)
24 West 40th Street, New York 18, New York

D. VAN NOSTRAND COMPANY, LTD.

358, Kensington High Street, London, W.14, England

D. VAN NOSTRAND COMPANY (Canada), LTD.

25 Hollinger Road, Toronto 16, Canada

Published simultaneously in Canada by
D. VAN NOSTRAND COMPANY (Canada), LTD.

Library of Congress Catalogue Card No. 59-14614

This book is one of the volumes in *The Asia Library,* a
series initiated by The Asia Society, Inc., a non-profit, non-
political, membership association whose purpose is to help
bring the people of America and Asia closer together in
their appreciation of each other and each other's way of life.

04603a25

PRINTED IN THE UNITED STATES OF AMERICA
BY LANCASTER PRESS, INC., LANCASTER, PA.

Foreword

According to Charles Doughty, his classic *Arabia Deserta* was written not because he had any preconceived interest in the country, but solely because he needed a subject for a book "that should redeem the English language from the slough into which it has fallen since the time of Spenser". Of the many good reasons for writing about a place, this is no doubt one of the best; and it is with regret that the author of the following brief sketch is obliged to disclaim any comparable motives. What occasioned this handbook for mid-twentieth century Thailand was merely that, during the four years when the author was stationed there as representative for The Asia Foundation, visitors often asked for a small, informal and unpretentious book about the country that would provide general information for the casual reader. While there were first-rate histories, personal memoirs and other specialized treatments, no such volume existed. Accordingly, when The Asia Society graciously suggested that he try to remedy the lack, there was a strong temptation to accept the invitation.

There were, of course, also good grounds for resisting the temptation. For one thing, many others had better qualifications for the task. For another, spending four years in a country is by no means the best way to prepare for writing about it. The traveller who writes after four weeks has the advantage of being able to utilize his first impressions, of being able to plead justifiable ignorance when found in error—as well as of close ties with his audience at home. A residence of forty years may well provide compensatory assets. What overcame the reluctance induced by these considerations was mainly that, in four years, one can acquire, if not erudition about a country, at least a lasting affection for it. The desire to provide some evidence, however inadequate, of this seemed reason enough for trying to write something about Thailand.

Comment should perhaps be made upon the use of Thai proper names and other words in the material that follows. Since there are several systems of transliteration, none of which is unanimously accepted, the best and easiest rule to follow seemed to be that of common usage. Accordingly, most place-names follow the spelling in popular maps; names of people the spelling apparently preferred by the bearers; and other words the spelling most frequently encountered. Thai words have usually been italicized—and, when necessary, translated—the first time they appear, but not thereafter.

Contents

Contents

1. The Place

Thailand (pronounced Tie-land), formerly known as Siam and still sometimes so-called by Thais or Siamese who may regard the new name as an unseemly innovation and who among themselves refer to it as *Muang Thai* (Land of the Free), is a small, torrid, and agreeable Southeast Asian kingdom about the size of France. Comprising an area of some 200,000 square miles, from North 5° 30″ to 21° and from East 97° 30″ to 105° 30″, the country is bounded, proceeding counterclockwise from the South, by the Gulf of Siam, Cambodia, Laos, Burma and Malaya. In shape, it bears a dim but appropriate resemblance to an elephant's profile, with its floppy left ear represented by the Northeast portion that extends into Laos, and its trunk by the Southern portion that curls three quarters of the way down the Malay Peninsula. The Northeast portion of the country is hilly, dry and poor. The Southern or peninsular part is sandy, mountainous and rich, especially in tin and rubber. The two other topographical divisions of Thailand are the North, celebrated for hill tribes, teak forests, and intermittently cool weather; and the Central Plain, where nearly half of Thailand's twenty-three million people pursue a way of life which contrasts pleasantly with that of their less fortunately situated Southeast Asian neighbors.

One thing that makes life agreeable for dwellers on the Central Plain of Thailand is the abundance of food, mainly rice, that grows there. The Central Plain consists chiefly of alluvial mud bordering the Menam (River) Chao Phraya (Senior Lord) which, as its name suggests, is to Thailand more or less what the Mississippi, or Old Man, River is to the U. S. Entirely flat, green as a leaf and rarely more than a few feet above sea level, the central plain is elaborately veined by a system of canals for irrigation and drainage. These canals, called *klongs,* add further to the congeniality of living arrangements for its residents in several ways. For one thing, most klongs are full of pan-sized fish which, readily extracted by line, net or trap according to the fisherman's whim, constitute an agreeable dietary accompaniment to the rice, which is

2

of an especially delectable variety. For another, they serve as highways upon which it is possible to travel, with a minimum of effort, in canoe-like *sampans*. Finally, the klongs are used both for bathing and as a source of drinking water. This provides Thais with a continuous oral vaccine which builds up their resistance to the germs, viruses, and microbes which thrive on the swampy, torrid Central Plain as handily as do the humans.

The final enhancement of existence for dwellers on the Central Plain, or indeed almost anywhere else in Thailand, is the climate which, while it may remind some visitors of the interior of a steam-laundry, especially in the rainy season, makes it practical for acclimated residents to exist with a minimum of fuss and bother and helps to render poverty not merely painless but often positively pleasant. The Siamese calendar is traditionally supposed to comprise three seasons: hot, from February through May; rainy, from June through October; and cool from November through January. In fact, while such distinctions are conspicuous to the highly sensitized Thais, they often seem a bit blurred to European visitors. Even in the rainy season, when as many as four or five usually brief torrential showers may fall in a single day, the weather remains sunny, and not much cooler than ninety, most of the time; and even in the cool season, when Thais are likely to bundle up in sweaters and woolen clothes, the

3

daytime temperature rarely drops much below seventy-five.

One of the advantages of such a climate is that the fewer clothes one has, or at least wears, the more comfortable one usually is. Another is that adequate shelter involves nothing much more than a rainproof roof, which can be readily fabricated out of palm-thatch. With the problems of shelter, clothing, and food reduced to a minimum, it is perhaps not altogether surprising that for Thais the attitude of calm acceptance of whatever fate may bring prescribed by the national religion of Buddhism is not, as a rule, especially difficult to maintain. This trait too helps to make Thailand eminently agreeable for visitors as well as for the residents themselves and is conspicuous enough to be reflected even in the titles of books about it, like *Thailand, Land of Smiles* by William Afred Rae Wood, a well-known historian who settled down in Thailand some years ago after completing a long and distinguished local career in the British consular service.

While Thailand's temperamental and topographical advantages might well be sufficient in themselves to set it far apart from its less favored neighbors, there are also other circumstances which, especially at present, give the nation an even stronger claim to notice. One of these is the fact that, unlike all the other countries in the area, and indeed practically all of Asia except China and Japan, Thailand has never been a colony

4

of any European power. Another is the corollary point that it is the only country in the area not now laboriously involved in acquiring the basic rudiments of self-government, Thailand's politicians having long since become adept practitioners of this art. The third and most important is that Thailand has always been wholly and enthusiastically committed to the free world in the twentieth century's global struggle against Communist aggression.

Thailand's commitment to the free world, which dates back at least to the time when the U.S. itself first took note of the existence of the Cold War, follows partly from the two other circumstances mentioned and partly from certain even more fundamental factors in the nation's history and character which can be examined presently. Meanwhile, the country's importance to world strategy can be perceived from a glance at the map, in which its geographical significance as the hub of its area is immediately apparent; and the sincerity of Thailand's sentiments can be deduced from, among other things, its promptness both in sending volunteers to Korea and in becoming the permanent headquarters of the Southeast Asia Treaty Organization (SEATO). However, before going into the question of Thailand's present role in world affairs, it may be appropriate to give further consideration to the precise nature of the nation's well-being, of which this role is to some degree both consequence and cause.

5

In appraising Thailand's well-being, it may be permissible to introduce a few relevant statistics. Instead of being over-crowded, like much of Asia, Thailand averages only one hundred and fourteen persons to the square mile; and since most of the miles are highly productive ones, it is, in fact, relatively empty. Virgin land is available and can still be secured from the government, as in Alaska; by using this, and with improved farming methods, Thailand could no doubt support fifty or seventy-five million residents even more comfortably than its present population. Currently between eighty-five and ninety percent of Thais are farmers and of these the majority own their own land —on the average, which is the largest in Asia, fifteen acres to a family. Eighteen million acres, or ninety percent of those which are arable, are planted in rice; of Thailand's remaining one hundred and twenty-five million acres, seventy-five million are forests which, on the wooded slopes North of the central plain, provide insurance against more severe flooding than the present seasonal overflow which makes the rice-farming practicable; and fifty million are desert, scrub, and marshland. The Thai rice crop averages some eight million tons a year, of which the twenty or so percent exported brings in about a hundred and fifty million dollars a year and is the major factor in the normally favorable Thai trade balance. Other substantial crops are rubber, tobacco and sugar—600,000, 100,000 and 50,000 acres respectively. Thais measure land in *rai*—a rai is .395 acres—and money in *baht* or *ticals*. The latter terms are synonymous; and a tical is a nickel, though the approximate rhyme is a better guide to value than to correct pronunciation, wherein the accent is on the final syllable.

Next to rice in the value of Thai exports come rubber ($75,000,000), tin ($25,000,000) and teak, of which the annual average value is more difficult to determine. Once second only to rice as an export, Thailand's teak, of which some 75,000 tons are produced and some 40,000 exported annually, represents the major source of world supply. It is also another one of the factors that help make its terrain profitable not only for its human residents but also for an unusually wide and spectacular array of other fauna. One reason that the map of Thailand's resemblance to the cranium of an elephant—perhaps really rather that of some toothless prehistoric mastodon than of a healthy modern tusker —seems appropriate is that Thailand is one of the few countries where elephants are still actually used for industrial purposes. In the teak forests of the North various kinds of mechanical tractors, bull-dozers and baggage-hoists have been tried for the tricky chore of picking up huge logs, nudging them through the underbrush and shunting them into the streams which send them, via the Menam Chao Phraya, down to Bangkok, whence they are exported to the rest of the world for boat decks, salad bowls and furniture. Elephants, of which there are several thousand in the Thai labor force, do the job much better.

As befits skilled workers in one of the nation's major industries, Thailand's teak elephants work short hours —five a day—are highly educated and even have a language of their own, which is common also to elephants and elephant trainers in Burma and Cambodia, some of whose pachyderms pursue similar lines of livelihood. Most Thai elephant trainers, starting in young, try to get animals of about the same age as themselves who will then provide a source of income for the remainder of both members' lifetimes in a sort of partnership arrangement not altogether unlike that provided in the U.S. by membership in a good brokerage or law firm. White elephants—scrupulously defined as elephants which, while rarely much lighter in general color than the rest of their species, are characterized by certain albino features, including those of the most intimate character—are regarded in Thailand as extremely lucky. All wild elephants are considered to belong to the Crown—as are all wild swans in England. White elephants are presented to the King as soon as they are found, as are all British sturgeon to the reigning monarch.

Next to its elephants, the most engaging animals in Thailand are doubtless its monkeys who also practice a profession—in their case, that of coconut picking, as conducted in the Southern portion of the peninsula. Coconut monkeys, like teak elephants, serve a long apprenticeship and are expected to be faultless in performance of their duties. Whenever a monkey picks a coconut which his master has instructed him to leave on the tree, he descends to the ground and presents his posterior for a spanking which, however much a kindly owner may regret it, must be administered immediately and always, if the creature is to retain the rigid discipline essential to his valued calling. The conventional Thai beast of burden is, of course, as in most other Southeast Asian countries, not the horse, which is sometimes used for transportation but more generally for racing or police work, but the water buffalo, usually tended on Thai farms by the pre-adolescent offspring of the owner. In present times of increasing road and automotive traffic, as distinguished from old-fashioned traffic on the klongs by sampan, water buffalos and motorists constitute a grave mutual hazard, especially at night. Some enterprising Thai farmers have lately tried to minimize this by pasting danger-signs on the hindquarters of their draft animals, in Scotchlite.

Also noteworthy in the directory of Thai fauna are some of its less congenial components including crocodiles, which are made into bags, belts, and spectacle-cases; small, drowsy bears, which amble about the woods, nibbling local plants including the opium-poppy; and tigers, which can be hunted either on the peninsula or in the northern hills. More likely to be encountered than these three are the poisonous snakes with which Thailand also regrettably abounds. Most deadly of Thailand's snakes is neither the cobra, whose bite will often prove fatal if not promptly treated, nor the larger king cobra, of whose bite the same is more emphatically true and who will go out of his way to inflict it, but rather the banded krait. Other species of poisonous snakes have venom which affects either the heart or the nervous system. The krait has venom which affects both, and which, if efficiently enough injected, is almost sure to be fatal unless treated within a few minutes.

The presence of all these lethal serpents is not so grave a menace as the uninitiated might suppose. Both kinds of cobras shun densely populated areas and move about mostly from twilight to dawn; the formidable krait is actually a torpid little wiggler who spends his days in stupor and even at night requires a sharp kick or a heavy foot-step to stir him to retaliatory action. Furthermore, an effective antidote to such menace as exists is furnished by Bangkok's Pasteur Institute, which is one of the most efficient and advantageously located anti-snake-bite-serum-producing establishments in the world. Herein anti-toxin, for export as well as home use, is produced from the blood of horses or sheep who have been mildly injected with venom from the copious coils of captive kraits and cobras. One of the more popular spectacles which Bangkok provides for its numerous tourists is that of the bi-weekly attentions paid to these caged monsters by their blasé keepers who grab them by their necks, squeeze the venom out of their fangs, squirt huge syringes of milk down their throats, and then toss them back to squirm into the moist trenches or dark cubbyholes where they prefer to doze away the hours.

About twenty miles up the Chao Phraya from its mouth, Bangkok, the capital of Thailand, is a booming city of a million and a half whose airport of *Don Muang* is rapidly becoming the major air-lane crossing of Southeast Asia. From Don Muang, serviced by eighteen airlines, it is possible to reach Rangoon in just over one hour, Singapore in about four, Hong Kong in five and Tokyo or Ceylon overnight. It is sometimes also possible, during the hours of peak traffic, to spend an hour and a half on the fifteen-mile highway between Don Muang and the heart of Bangkok. The heart of Bangkok, an area hard to define satisfactorily, is represented for most visitors by New Road—so-called because, when it was built a hundred or so years ago to connect the custom house with the business district a mile or so further up the left bank of the stream, it was the city's second paved thoroughfare. New Road traffic involves *samlors,* or three wheeled pedicabs, the most cosmopolitan imaginable mixture of conventional cars and a clutch of ancient trolleys which move in both directions on a single-track line through a district which includes most of Bangkok's tourist shops. At the river-end of an intersecting lane stands the Oriental Hotel which was once the scene of a fortunate convalescence by W. Somerset Maugham, some of whose subsequent stories use Thailand as a background, as do some of Joseph Conrad's. Bangkok means "water-flower village"; Thais also refer to it as "Krung-thep," meaning "City of Angels," or Los Angeles.

From the point of view of governmental, cultural or religious affairs, the heart of Bangkok is a less congested area at the opposite, or up-river, end of town, occupied mainly by palaces, government bureaus, monuments, edifices housing offices of international organizations like SEATO or UNESCO, and, most impressive of all, the magnificent *chedis* of Bangkok's major *wats,* or Buddhist monasteries, upon which Maugham's apt comment in the *Gentleman in the Parlour* was as follows: "It makes you laugh with delight to think that anything so fantastic could exist on this sombre earth. . . . The artists who developed them step by step from the buildings of the Ancient Khmers had the courage to pursue their fantasy to the limit. . . ." *Chedi* is a term which, while applicable to any religious memorial, most often means a bell-shaped tower. Somewhat similar terms sometimes confused with it are *stupa,* which means more or less the same thing except that when used of a structure it is less definitive as to shape; and *prang,* a word of Khmer origin which applies properly to a Khmer-style tower.

Between the government side of the city and the New Road area but further inland from the river lie the sprawling, leafy, residential regions that make Bangkok, despite its humid heat, an eminently pleasant capital in which to live; while enclosed by all three areas, and on the fourth side by a deep bend in the river, lies the teeming commercial heart of the town. Populated largely by Chinese, of whom Thailand contains some three million and Bangkok almost a third of the total, this area is a hive of frame shops, swarming block-tenements and all manner of refreshment dispensaries, from mobile sidewalk-kitchens to elaborate restaurant dance halls, such as the renowned four-storey *Hoi Thien Lao.* Also included until rather recently were legal opium dens which constituted testimony to Thai tolerance and common sense, since drug addiction is a less pressing problem in Bangkok than in, say, Boston.

Across the Chao Phraya River from Bangkok on the right or West bank is the suburb of Thonburi, technically a separate municipality, whose warehouses, lumberyards, and boat-sheds are criss-crossed by even busier klongs than those which also intersect Bangkok itself in all directions. On the big klongs of Thonburi,

13

traffic-density exceeds that normally in evidence on the Grand Canal of Venice, a metropolis to which Bangkok has often been compared and whose celebrated gondolas may well derive from the same source as its ancient sampans, adapted in the course of transit via the coast of India, the Red Sea and the Mediterranean. Down the meandering river from Bangkok, ten miles by water or five by land on the same or East side stands the New Port, or Customs Area, where most ships now load and unload, either directly onto the docks or by lighter while anchored in the stream. Although most of Thailand's imports come from, and exports go to, other parts of the Far East and Europe, the U.S. is the nation's biggest single customer and supplier, buying over fifty million dollars worth a year and selling almost forty.

Although Bangkok stands to other cities of Thailand somewhat as Paris does to the other cities of France, dwarfing them in population, influence and other aspects, this does not imply that Thailand's provincial towns are lacking in special interest, which is perhaps increased by contrast. Next to Bangkok, the most noteworthy is the Northern metropolis of Chiengmai, once the capital of an independent principality, whose former ruling dynasty has been amiably absorbed into the Thai peerage. Situated in a wide and fertile river-valley between wooded Northern hills, and so much cooler than Bangkok that frosts have been reported and an

icicle was even rumored to have formed on one
legendary winter night, Chiengmai has a population of
some fifty thousand engaged, among other things, in
molding or hammering silver of a special alloy, carving
teak statuary, and making decorative umbrellas out of
painted paper.

More or less what Chiengmai is to the North of
Thailand, the busy commercial town of Songkhla, Thailand's second largest port, is to the tin-mining and
rubber-raising area of the Peninsula. Major towns of
the Northeast are Nakhon Ratchasima, Udon, and
Ubon, where the Thai Government and UNESCO
jointly maintain a Fundamental Education Center.
Other towns of some historical, political or commercial
interest are Nakhon Pathom, which has the biggest
chedi in the land and, with the possible exception of
Rangoon's Shwedagon Pagoda, in the world; Nongkhai, across the Mekong (which is the world's seventh
largest river) from the Laotian capital of Vientiane;
and Fang, a Northern outpost, where an ooze of surface oil may or may not betoken substantial deposits
further down. Ayudhya, forty or so miles north of
Bangkok, was the capital of Siam until the Burmese
sacked it in 1767, thus causing the government to move
first to Thonburi and, a few years later on, to Bangkok.
Its noteworthy ruins have lately been subjected to
somewhat ostentatious renovation.

Two other areas often unjustifiably omitted from

catalogs of Thailand's metropolitan assets are the agreeable shore resorts of Bangsaen and Hua Hin, on the East and West shores respectively of the Bight of Bangkok. Bangsaen, about two hours drive from Bangkok, is the handier of the two but Hua Hin, about one hundred and fifty miles Southwest of the capital, where the Royal Family have their summer residence and a first-rate golf course winds into the craggy wooded hills, is perhaps even more attractive. The elite of Thailand like to spend the "hot months" of March and April at Hua Hin in wooden villas or cottages or at the capacious Hua Hin Hotel, all of which confront shining crescents of talcum-powder, surf-soaped beach.

Some eighty or more percent of the people of Thailand live not in its towns and cities but in its forty thousand or so small villages, which on the populous central plain are most often built along the sides of klongs, with rice fields stretching back from the houses. According to anthropological studies, these agreeable settlements, of three hundred to three thousand people each, are divided into three types, strip-villages, cluster-villages, and dispersed-villages, according to their ground plan. In any case, each has its wat whose towers can be discerned from afar, above the dense foliage of flowering shade trees. Formerly connected with each other mainly by waterways, Thai villages are now often linked also by rail and by a highway system of which the main arteries are hardtop roads converging on Bangkok from termini at Hua Hin, Nongkhai and Fang.

Living conditions in Thai villages vary sufficiently from region to region and time to time to make most generalizations about them unreliable if not misleading. A few that may perhaps be permissible concern village dwellings which are usually built on four- to five-foot stilts for flood-protection, with thatched roofs and comfortable verandas. Each house is at or near the center of its fenced compound which contains a vegetable garden, fruit trees, and a spirit house. Thai houses usually have an odd-number of rooms, for good luck, and they may cost the equivalent of ten to five hundred dollars, depending on size, materials, and the type of labor employed in the construction. In most Thai village households, the wife and daughters attend to cooking, washing, and tidying up; husband and sons do most of the farm work except at periods of peak activity, when everyone pitches in. Shoes are never worn in the house—nor, so far as that goes, outdoors either a good part of the time; and furniture is at a sensible minimum. Latrines and bathing facilities—the latter comprising a shoulder-high screen of thatch surrounding a water-jug, if the compound does not border on a klong—are outside the house. Chickens and pigs, if any, make their headquarters in the open area under the floor where appropriate scraps can be swept, tossed or handed down to them in orderly and effortless fashion.

Thai village customs in regard to child-bearing, courtship, marriage, divorce, death, funerals, work, play, worship and all the other business and ceremony of existence have been exhaustively studied and ably described in such works as *Village Life in Modern Thailand* by John deYoung or *Siamese Rice Village,* by an expert group of Thailand specialists at Cornell University. Above these villages nowadays fly huge international airliners and the planes of the Thai Airways by means of which all major cities and areas of the nation are readily accessible from Bangkok. From the air, the green plains of Thailand stretch to the horizons like a wide calm sea, in which signs of life are rarely discernible. This impression is, of course, erroneous. Thai people are a lively group, up to all manner of commotion.

2. The People

In the opinion of many commentators, Thais are, by and large, the handsomest people in the Orient. Small, slight, and delicately built, they are usually darker than Chinese, with small bones, well-made torsos and attractive faces. Thai women especially are often extravagantly graceful and good-looking. Young Thai girls are expected to be proficient in the national idiom of the dance, which stresses manual gesticulation, and are likely to spend their spare moments practicing it. As a result, most of them have unusually graceful hands, with tapering fingers flexible enough to bend backwards at a ninety-degree angle.

The dexterity of Thai women is by no means exclusively digital; they seem expert also at most of the numerous activities they undertake, including business, the professions, and the arts. In distinction from women elsewhere in Asia, who are often obliged to lead an emphatically domestic life, as in Japan or in the Middle East, those of Southeast Asia have been traditionally more versatile. One of the subsidiary temples near Angkor Wat—two hours flight from Bangkok, which is the usual port of access to this twelfth-century Cambodian marvel—was reputedly constructed entirely by women. Thai women, in line with hallowed precedent, are still widely employed in the building of roads, houses, and temples, most often as hod-carriers or masons. Those in higher income or education brackets may become lawyers, doctors, or experts at sports like golf, badminton, and tennis, much less in consequence of the recent emancipation that started in Europe with the present century than of a millennium of local example. Thai women write books, edit magazines and sculpt; they own property, often in large holdings, and are adept at counselling their husbands on business and all other matters.

Thai men and women generally enjoy verbal humor, most especially verbal humor of a satiric sort involving puns, persiflage and plays on words. Thais, either of the same or opposite sexes, sometimes hold hands while walking, but otherwise avoid conspicuous mutual contact. The Thai salutation is the *wai,* made by putting the palms and fingers of both hands together and raising them to the face in the gesture of Christian prayer with which it may well have some common Indo-European derivation. The wai is accompanied by a bow and a smile, the width of the latter and the depth of the former being largely determined by the relative age and status of the participants. Thais are not enthusiastic about shaking hands and dislike being touched on the head for any reason whatsoever. Nothing seems ruder to a Thai than to be grabbed by the arm, clapped on the back or otherwise mauled in the boisterous fashion employed by some Westerners to express amiability. Many old-fashioned Thais enjoy chewing betel-nut; elderly Thai women often wear their hair *en brosse* or even in crew-cuts, a fashion consequent, according to legend, upon the Burmese invasion of 1767, when numerous Thai girls were summarily dragged off by their topknots.

In explaining many of the numerous differences between the behavior of Thais and that of the inhabitants of the rest of the world one point to keep in mind is that, as previously noted, Thailand is unique among the countries of Southeast Asia in that it has never been a European colony. As to why Thailand was an exception to the rule in this respect, there are several schools of thought; the results are much less controversial. These are that Thais, unlike most other Southeast Asians, are untouched by any trace of what the psychiatrists call *trauma* where Europeans are concerned. They treat visitors with neither resentment nor exaggerated respect but rather with a gracious air of quiet curiosity, which makes their guests feel flattered and at ease. More important than its effects upon contemporary tourists have been the consequences of this attitude toward visitors upon Thailand's own colorful history, both early and contemporary.

Almost as intimately and extensively concerned with the peculiarities of Thai character and behavior as this unique feature of its political annals is, no doubt, its religion. In Thailand, where Buddhism is practiced as widely and diligently as Roman Catholocism is in Italy or Spain, young men are more or less expected at some time or other to pass a few days, weeks, or months in a monastery. This brief dip into the contemplative life, along with emphasis upon Buddhist teaching at home and in school, tends to inculcate a benign imperturbability which, while neither impenetrable nor universal, is a clearly marked national trait which distinguishes Thais from most Europeans and even from most other Asians. Excitable Caucasians of various types who stay in Thailand for any length of time are likely to find themselves talking in lower tones of voice, walking with a more deliberate gait, and even brushing a bug off a coat-sleeve instead of squashing it. Such responses are, of course, well suited to a tropical environment from the hygienic as well as from the philosophical viewpoint.

A final factor that no doubt helps to explain some facets of Thai conduct is the upbringing and family life customary in most parts of the country. Thai convention, as audiences at the stage or screen versions of *The King and I* were made thoroughly aware, used to condone plural marriage. While really grand-scale polygamy was never prevalent outside of court or the upper-upper strata of Thai society, if only for economic reasons, and while even small-scale polygamy is nowadays less widely practiced, it is true that family life at all levels of Thai society retains a flexibility that is usually lacking in most other Western or even Asian societies. Thai husbands may, and often do, even nowadays, have second or third wives, if they so desire; in any case, they do not necessarily feel obliged to practice, or even to affect, the sort of connubial fidelity customary in most Western countries.

Thai families in villages are usually related to numerous other families in the same area; consanguine groups mingle on easy terms, so that young children—who venerate parents and grand-parents more than is conventional in the West—may venerate several sets of them, and be as intimate with several sets of cousins as with their own brothers and sisters. In towns and cities, various representatives of three or even four generations may inhabit the same family compound, using the same house, several houses, or both schemes interchangeably. In adult life, many members of the

Thai elite occupy two or more jobs, often holding down a government post in the morning, a private one in the afternoon and a university lectureship between times. According to one learned Thai psychiatrist, this may be less because of the economic or social pressures to which the habit is usually attributed than merely because having two or more sets of parent-substitutes reproduces in an agreeable way the pleasurable plethora to which they become accustomed in the much relished period of childhood.

Whatever may be the mainsprings of Thai behavior patterns, these are in any case engaging enough to provide ample scope for research by psychiatrists, philosophers, social scientists, or all three together. As good an example of this as any other is the one which first confronts the visitor, i.e., the Thai language. This resembles Chinese, in that it employs disparate tones to differentiate between words which would otherwise sound identical. The troublesome syllable *ma,* for example, can mean "dog," "horse," or "come," depending upon whether it is said in a rising, high-level or middle-level tone respectively. Instead of being written in Chinese characters, however, Thai uses a unique alphabet of Sanskritic origin, in which the consonants are written on one line with various marks above, below, before or after to indicate the vowel-sounds that follow them. Most common Thai words are peculiar to Thai; a minority derive from Chinese or Sanskrit which occupy an etymological relationship in Thai somewhat analogous to that of Anglo-Saxon and Latin in English, to which Thai's remote relationship shows up from time to time in common root-words. An example is the astonishingly ubiquitous suffix "buri," meaning town or place. This suffix, as used in Thai place-names like Thonburi or Chantaburi, is etymologically as well as phonetically identical with the same word as used in English "Danbury" or "Canterbury," and also, for that matter, related to the "burgh" of Edinburgh, the "pore" of Singapore, the "pur" of Jodpur and the "borough" or "burrow" of Brooklyn or a rabbit.

Even stranger perhaps than the intrinsic characteristics of the Thai language are the extrinsic ones which become apparent when efforts are made to transliterate it into English, which is widely spoken in Thailand and is a required subject in Thai schools. At least a dozen diverse methods for transliteration have been devised in the century or so since the need for them arose. Since several of these achieved partial, but none of them complete, acceptance, and since usage also affects the matter, the net result can perhaps best be judged from one or two well-known proper names where the problem is perhaps most dramatically and conveniently exemplified. The most celebrated prime minister of Thailand during the present century was no doubt the one deposed in 1957, who was and is usually referred to in the press as Field Marshal P. Phibul Songgram. "Phibul," as he was called in headlines—Thai last names are rarely used and people are conventionally addressed or alluded to by their first ones—is also permissibly spelled "Phibun" or "Pibul," but pronounced Peeboon, in accord with the rule that "ph" equals "p," "i" equals "ee" and "l" at the end of a Thai name is always pronounced like "n." An even better case-study might be Phibul's successor as Thailand's major political figure, Field Marshal Sarit Thanarat, whose first name is pronounced in accord with this spelling but spelled, by some transliterational purists, as "Srishti." Instances of this sort are so frequent that Thai nomenclature rivals English nomenclature in its phonetic eccentricity.

As to Thai cookery, which is a combination of Chinese and Indian retaining the spicier features of both, it employs, along with a rice basis, the curry of India and the condiments of China, and has a quality of its own which occasionally makes the neophyte gourmet suspect that he has swallowed a napalm bomb. In ordinary farm or family style Thai cooking, the fundamental staples of rice and fish are usually accompanied by various peppery pastes and sauces. In urban restaurants or elegant households a vast array of other ingenious concoctions supplements these staples, some bland and many fiery. Fortunately for those western visitors who may prefer a less incandescent diet, Thai housecooks who may be employed for thirty dollars a month and up, are quite competent to supply it. Likewise fortunately, the Thai menu provides what may well be the world's most diversified and delectable assortment of fruits, including the finest imaginable mangoes, the flavorsome durian and more than two dozen different, and delicious, species of banana. European restaurants, including French, Hungarian, and even dairy-style, abound in Bangkok along with Chinese ones, which are also plentiful in the provinces.

Thai clothes differ from Western ones, except in urban areas where many Thais have adopted the latter, in being considerably less cumbersome and accordingly better adapted to the prevailing weather. Thai farmers usually wear shirts, loose cotton trousers, and wide straw hats. The least dispensable item in Thai male attire is a piece of cotton cloth called a *pakoma* which may be worn as a turban, wound decoratively around the middle, or used as the wrapping for a bundle like the Japanese *furoshiki;* it may serve also as a bathcloth, a light covering to be used during catnaps, or even a lead-rope for a water-buffalo. Thai women wear wrap-around skirts called *pasin,* on the order of *sarongs* but longer, which are held in place by a gold or silver belt. Both Thai men and women preserve extreme modesty about display of their persons, which, combined with their healthy, sanitary, and comfortable habit of bathing several times a day in the convenient

27

klongs, has led to the development of remarkable virtuosity in personal concealment. Men conventionally effect this by means of the *pakoma* and women by means of the *pasin;* both can bathe in full view of the highway without revealing as much epidermis as is normally visible in a European drawing-room, not to mention a swimming-pool. Thai court-dress—consisting of a white silk tunic fastened by gold buttons up to a severe military collar, worn with a species of knickerbocker called *panung* made by looping a silk sarong around each leg and knotting it in back—is now largely out of fashion except among senior members of the royal family.

In an extended work about Thailand, Thai royalty and its own peculiarities would certainly deserve a chapter by itself. Until fairly recently, Thai monarchs were not only absolute but, at least theoretically, the most absolute in the world, not even excepting their Saudi Arabian or Manchu compeers. Kings were approached by their subjects on all fours. Their persons were regarded as so exalted that the penalty for touching one was death, also prescribed for persons who whispered during a royal audience, let a stray dog into the palace, or rocked a royal boat. When occasion for executing a royal personage arose, as sometimes occurred, he was enclosed in a red bag and placed upon ground covered by banana leaves, which are moisture-proof. A swift tap on the back of the neck then usually sufficed to dispose of him without noticable bloodshed. An even more dramatic demonstration of the sanctity of royal persons, and one which many contemporary residents of Bangkok have heard about from elderly eye witnesses, was provided in the latter part of the nineteenth century after a river collision involving a royal barge, when a Queen of Thailand was left to drown since, if one of the boatmen had saved her life by pulling her out, he would have been guilty of mortal *lèse majesté*.

More functional than the rules concerning the persons of Thai royalty are those pertaining to their offspring, especially in regard to titles. In a state where, until recent times, royalty was expected to practice polygamy in the fullest sense of the word, royal progeny were naturally only less numerous than the progeny of royal progeny. Had all such exalted individuals and all their descendants enjoyed the titles and prerogatives of princes, the business of the nation would have been seriously impeded. Thais, always practical and duly responsive to Buddhist concepts of the Golden Mean, solved this dilemma with characteristic ingenuity. According to Thai convention, somewhat simplified here for the sake of brevity, the son or daughter of a King and Queen is a Chao Fa (Royal Highness), that of a Chao Fo is a Pra Ong Chao (Royal Highness), his is a Mom Chao (Serene Highness), his is a Mom Rajawongse and his is a Mom

29

Luang. The child of a Mom Luang, however, is a mere commoner, so that even in ancient times the ranks of royalty were precluded from growing unmanageably crowded. Nowadays, when Thai kings practice monogamy, this Law of Diminishing Nobility ensures that the number of titled Thais will rapidly dwindle towards zero.

One difficulty in generalizing about the Thai national character is that, even more than in most other countries of the modern world, Thailand's population includes a wide spectrum of ethnic, religious, extranational, and linguistic subdivisions. Before the Thai arrived in Thailand, supposedly around 1000 A.D., the land was tenanted by Mon, Khmer, and earlier aboriginal inhabitants, some traces of whom still remain. More modern strains include the Chinese, usually estimated as 3,000,000, Malay (670,000), Cambodian or Vietnamese (200,000), Indian and Pakistani (60,000), some thirty assorted hill tribes (300,000) and itinerant Europeans (5,000), all of whom, except for some of the hill tribes, intermarry with Thais to a greater or less degree. Most influential of these groups, from the point of view of their standing in the Thai community, is doubtless the minuscule European element, most of whose members are diplomats, missionaries or traders, many of whom live on a comparatively lavish scale in Bangkok, hobnobbing with each other and the Thai upper-crust. Subdivided between

American, British, German and others, in approximately that numerical order, the foreign community has been warmly welcomed in Thailand for the last hundred years. Hospitable Thai governments have provided everything possible to make them comfortable, including a Royal Bangkok Sports Club where Europeans are invited by Thais to associate with them in the practice of a wide variety of outdoor and indoor diversions on a basis of complete equality.

Europeans of all nationalities are inclusively referred to in Thailand as *farangs*—a word of which the derivation may be either the word "Frank" as used by the Saracens in reference to the Crusaders and carried Eastward, via Persia and India through the centuries, or its derivative, the word "Français" as used in Southeast Asia from the 17th century on. Thai consideration for farangs is by no means confined to the recreational aspects of their existence. One of the titles of the King of Thailand is that of "Defender of Religion," meaning all religions, as distinct from the more limited British royal designation of "Defender of the Faith." With religious hospitality unequalled elsewhere on the terrestrial globe, the Thais consider religion in this sense to include not only their own but also that of all their alien guests. Christian missions in Thailand are accordingly as tax-free as Buddhist wats or, for that matter, Moslem mosques, and the King makes annual contributions to both Protestant and Catholic Christian churches as well as to the institutions of his own faith, with whose generous tenets such practices are compatible. In line with them likewise, Buddhist dignitaries may also be found among the members of Christian organizations, e.g. the Bangkok Y.M.C.A.

Thai hospitality to Europeans is equalled by that shown to most other racial groups. Malays congregate mainly in communities near the Southern border where they work in tin mines and on rubber plantations. Indians, of whom there are some 50,000, congregate in Bangkok where they dominate the textile industry as well as the popular calling of night watchman. Hindus have a meeting place of their own called the Thai-Bharata Lodge, where they can practice their rites without let or hindrance. Cambodians and Vietnamese are scattered about the Northeast, where even those of the latter who are refugee sympathizers with Ho Chi Minh are hospitably treated while being re-educated to a viewpoint more congenial with that of their new environment. Almost the only extra-national group in Thailand with whom friction ever arises are the Chinese; since these, however, form by far the largest single alien element, this unfortunate distinction is not one that can be readily ignored.

In considering the Chinese problem, as it is called in Thailand, the first point to bear in mind is that the figure of three million is misleading. The number of persons in Thailand who have one or more Chinese grand-parents might be larger by at least a million, while the number of pure Chinese who have not yet become Thai citizens is much smaller, perhaps not more than 500,000. Friction between Thai and Chinese in Thailand can scarcely be regarded as racial in character nor is it religious since the Chinese, so far as they have any religion at all, would probably have to be classed as some sort of fallen-away Buddhists and since all forms of Buddhism advocate tolerance in any case. It seems to reside primarily in the fact that the Chinese, despite their cleverness in other lines, have been slow to adopt Thai attitudes toward money, work, and competition. Unlike the Thais, the Chinese in Thailand show marked enthusiasm for getting ahead in the world on a monetary basis and for pecuniary occupations like banking, retail-trade, and rice-mills. Thai government policy toward the Chinese in Thailand has been, and is, to encourage their assimilation into the native population. The annual head tax upon aliens, which was raised from twenty baht to four hundred in 1952, has now been reduced from four hundred to two hundred, and heads of the various local associations of Chinese in Bangkok are currently on a satisfactory footing with Thai government, industrial, and social leaders. Thai prejudice toward the Chinese, which for a short time after World War II reached a degree of intensity almost reminiscent of the Nazi attitude toward Jews, is now much milder and less personal. Politically, some of the Thai Chinese favor the mainland government and some Taiwan—though in what proportion and with what intensity remains a moot question.

In addition to the various subdivisions of mortals in Thailand, the population may also be considered to include their invisible companions, first the *Theps,* or royal imported Hindu immortals for whom Krung-Thep was named, and second the more ordinary spirits who are commonly known as *phi.* Phi, of whom the most numerically substantial tribe are the *Pra Pum,* derive from pre-Buddhist beliefs of what sociologists describe as an animistic character. In modern Thailand, they are obviously just as much alive as they ever were and almost every well-appointed residence has its Pra Pum, or spirit, house—on a post in the front yard so situated that the shadow of the human house will never fall on it. Along with incense and joss-sticks, sustenance in the form of rice and fruit is placed in the Pra Pum house from time to time—as in the U. S. bits of bread or suet are placed in or near birdhouses which resemble them and which might, in point of fact, be traced down to similar atavistic sources. It is perhaps noteworthy that Thai birds, who are exceptionally tame and often alight on tables to peck at crumbs, rarely nest in houses that are occupied by Pra Pum.

3. Personages, Policies and Problems

No less noteworthy than the characteristics of the Thai people in general are those of Thai individuals in particular of whom many, past and present, not only rank high on the international scale for talent, originality and all around competence in their special fields but do so in a way that, like the nation's demographic characteristics, is special to Thailand. Two such individuals might be Prince Wan Waithiakon, the longtime Thai Foreign Minister, who was President of the United Nations General Assembly in 1955, and King Mongkut, the celebrated Thai monarch to whose mid-nineteenth century career a whole series of mid-twentieth century biographies in book, play, and cine-

35

matic format have failed to do the roughest sort of justice. Among younger contemporary Thai personages, a strong candidate for admission to this group might be Mom Rajawongse Kukrit Pramoj, one of the numerous great-grandsons of King Rama II, whose diverse credentials include being one of Thailand's foremost publishers, political commentators, and interpreters of the role of Ravana, the Demon King of Lanka, in the Thai dance-drama.

Among the theories advanced by M. R. Kukrit, whose versatility is regarded as remarkable in a land where a high degree of versatility is taken for granted, is one that concerns the historical position of Thailand between the Indo-Chinese colonies of France and the Indian, Malayan and Burmese ones of Britain. According to this theory, the British not only outwitted the French but also established themselves in Thailand far more effectively than in any of the Asian countries to which they took outright possession, by abstaining from any effort to do the latter. Instead of trying to conquer Thailand by force, which might have resulted in a war with France, the British succeeded in gaining the lasting friendship of the Thais by treating Thai royalty on a basis of equality, by entering into partnership arrangements with Thai commercial interests and, above all, by encouraging the Thai elite to send their offspring to British public schools and universities. So many Thai scions have attended Eton, Harrow, and

36

the like that, according to this well-qualified pundit, himself an old Oxonian, the name Thailand can best be justified by regarding it as an abbreviation of the phrase, "Old School Thailand."

In addition to indicating the correct pronunciation of the new name, this characteristically Kukritical observation may shed some oblique light on the question of Thailand's relations with the outside world in general and its role in Southeast Asia in particular. Adherence to British interests and, by extension, Western European ones, helps to explain Thailand's entrance into World War I, when a token force was dispatched to join the Allies. In World War II, Thailand, to be sure, declared war on Britain and the United States under the pressure of Japanese occupation but remained sufficiently aligned with her Western adversaries to provide them with a notably active Free Thai underground. Nowadays, the United Kingdom, where there are usually five hundred or more Thai students in residence, is rivalled in its prestige as an educational dispensary only by the U. S., where even more Thais go for schooling. The American University Alumni language-center in Bangkok teaches, to be sure, a species of colloquial Americanese which contrasts sharply with the more dulcet accents to be heard at the Old England Students' Association, but the annual festivities of the two organizations, involving dance-

37

bands and amateur theatricals, compete with each other as social attractions for the Thai aristocracy.

A criticism sometimes directed at Thailand by commentators in the stage of emergence from the colonial chrysalis is that Thais are actually less Asian in some aspects of their character and attitude than they are European. As evidence in support of this are cited both Thailand's commitment to the Free World and Bangkok's present eminence as the seat not only of the Southeast Asia Treaty Organization but also of a number of regional offices for United Nations Agencies including UNESCO and the World Health Organization. In actual fact, both the presence of such organizations in Bangkok and the trend of Thailand's foreign policy might perhaps better be interpreted as indications of Thailand's significance as a link not only between Europe and Southeast Asia but also, in a sense, between Southeast Asia's own past and present.

Whereas European nations, because as well as in spite of their quarrels with each other, have always remained a community whose members profited from inter-communication and awareness of each others' histories and characters, the nations of Southeast Asia, which once formed a similar community, abruptly ceased to do so during the age of colonization. During this period, they not only ceased to communicate with each other at all, except as subordinate appendages of European powers, but even lost track of their own histories as distinct from those of their distant alien proprietors in whose annals they were treated, often even in their own schools, as insignificant footnotes. Thailand, however, represents both a repository where the cultural traditions of Southeast Asia were able to survive unimpaired and a sanctuary in which its spiritual values were preserved intact.

The potential importance of Thailand in assisting the re-establishment of an Asian community, which thus starts with the unique assets provided by history, is increased further by those related qualifications conferred upon it by geography. Thailand's central location among the nations of the area is emphasized further by that of Bangkok as the natural hub of all air-routes in the region—south down the Malay Peninsula to Singapore and Jakarta, east to Hong Kong and Tokyo, or west to India and the Middle East—with New York about equidistant by either the eastern or the western route. Fully aware of its advantages in this respect, Bangkok is a hospitable, handsome and extraverted metropolis which gives every indication of welcoming the opportunity to become the major convention city of its area by constant enlargement of its already copious facilities for visitors. Bangkok's magnificent Sala Santhitham, or Peace Hall, which contains the offices of the Economic Commission for Asia and the Far East (ECAFE) and two large air-conditioned auditoriums equipped for instantaneous

39

translation, is possibly the most commodious institution of its sort west of San Francisco. The selection of Bangkok as the site of such cosmopolitan gatherings as the Ninth Pacific Science Congress in 1957 or the World Federation of Buddhists in 1958, and as the permanent site of such regional organizations as the Association of Southeast Asian Institutions of Higher Learning, is a noteworthy indication of its possible future development in this direction.

For Thailand as for every other nation of Southeast Asia, or for that matter the entire free world, a crucial problem nowadays is, of course, that of Communism and how best to deal with it. Thailand's position on the Communist time-table may well be conditioned by the facts that it is ringed by other countries which might, for various reasons, be considered to be easier game, and that, if some or all of them fell, Thailand might be expected to do likewise. In any event, members of Thailand's four Communist parties —Thai, Chinese, Vietnamese and Malayan, all of which are illegal—have not to date displayed either the energy or the ingenuity that has characterized the efforts of their confreres in some neighboring areas. However, to say that the efforts of the Communists in Thailand are not quite up to the regional standard by no means indicates that they are entirely without resources or the ability to utilize them.

Major targets of Communist subversion in Thailand

for the past few years have been (a) the Overseas Chinese and (b) the press, both Thai and Chinese. Activities in connection with the latter have traditionally been conducted—since Thailand maintains diplomatic relations with Taiwan rather than mainland China—through the Soviet Embassy, many of whose staff members, in contrast with their U. S. confreres, speak at least adequate Thai. A prime factor in Communist selection of the Thai press as a high priority target is no doubt its susceptibility to financial inducement. Bangkok, which is the only city big enough to have any daily papers at all, has a total of around thirty of which a score or so are in Thai, and the rest in Chinese or English. More relevant than the complex cause of this journalistic surplus may be its economic consequence: since none of the Thai papers has a circulation of more than twenty thousand, and most have less than ten, editorial salaries are at a minimum and reporters are under pressure to accept outside sources of income. However, whatever adverse effects the influence of the Thai press may have had upon its readers is doubtless mitigated by the fact that, according to a recent survey, reporters rank barely ahead of politicians on the scale of popular prestige.

Until 1958, when Field Marshal Sarit banned imports from Communist China, Thailand had for several years been swamped with mainland products, funneled through Hong Kong. Even apparently nonideological items, such as toys, thermos bottles, sewing machines and bicycles, had a considerable impact beyond the commercial, because they undersold competing merchandise even from Japan and thus gave a false impression of mainland industrial prowess. Ideological imports included books, magazines, and movies in large quantities. As elsewhere in Southeast Asia, mainland Chinese films have the initial advantage of being made for an audience of 600,000,000 which permits far more expensive production than can be practicable among non-Communist impresarios in Hong Kong or Taiwan who have only the marginal audience of 13,000,000 or so Overseas Chinese and 10,000,000 Taiwanese to aim at. An additional and, one might think, superfluous advantage, though not one which the Communist distributors are prone to overlook, is government subsidies to guarantee profits to exhibitors, for showing their wares, along with bribes to exclude those of their competitors. Mainland movies, moreover, are often so skillfully written and directed that the nature of their message frequently seemed to escape Thai government officials, whose job was to keep Communist propaganda out.

Even more conspicuous in Thailand than their success with movies among the Overseas Chinese has been the Communists' success in the field of education which, as in other countries, is a major area for their interest. Chinese children in Thailand are permitted to attend

Chinese primary schools up to the age of about fourteen when they transfer to Thai secondary schools, in line with the Government policy of encouraging assimilation. Communist agents have circumvented this arrangement by organizing evening "study groups" which at once evade the government definition of "schools" and ensure individual attention for each scholar by remaining within the statutory minimum of seven pupils each. Such study groups use textbooks which, printed in Hong Kong, maintain strict adherence to the party line and are designed not only for local effect but also as preparatory schools for colleges and universities on the mainland—since Chinese college-level instruction is not available in Thailand nor anywhere else in Southeastern Asia except Singapore or Hong Kong. Chinese students who wish to continue their studies in their native tongue, and who choose mainland colleges in preference to the more limited free world facilities, can be, and presumably often are, later smuggled back into Thailand as adult agents.

Communist efforts in Thailand are by no means unopposed, both by the Thai government and also by its interested allies. The U. S., in addition to a well-staffed Embassy, maintains an Information Service, a Joint U. S. Military Advisory Group and a busy International Cooperation Administration Mission, which disburses aid at an average rate of some $25,000,000 a year on projects in the fields of agriculture, health, edu-

43

cation, economics, and engineering. In the last category a major item is the "Friendship Road," to improve communications throughout the Northeast and the Central Plain—which will also profit greatly from the hundred million dollar Yanhee Dam, financed in part by a sixty-six million dollar World Bank loan, to provide important new facilities for flood control and irrigation. On the educational front, the ICA Mission—in Thailand called U. S. Operations Mission, or USOM—sends some four hundred government officials and others to the U. S. every year and through contracts with U. S. universities, notably Indiana, Oregon State, Wayne State, and Texas, brings advisory groups to Thai institutions of higher learning in Bangkok, where they co-operate with Thai faculty members to raise the teaching level and broaden the curricula. Such institutions also profit from exchanges of professors and students financed under the Fulbright and Smith-Mundt Acts. Meanwhile military aid, as administered through JUSMAG, has provided the Thai armed forces, totaling some 300,000, with up-to-date training and equipment including an appropriate quota of jet fighterplanes for which the Thais provide able pilots.

USOM aid to Thailand, since 1950, has amounted to some one hundred and seventy million dollars, not counting the hundred or so million dollars worth of local currency provided by the Thais themselves. Among the tangible results have been anti-malaria and

44

yaws campaigns which have practically eradicated these diseases; five thousand miles or so of farm-to-market highways; four hundred or so new or improved bridges over klongs or rivers; elimination of the bar at the mouth of the Chao Phraya River, to permit the entrance of bigger ships; enlargement of some 30,000 kilowatts in urban generating capacity; major improvements in rice-growing techniques; and other similar benefits far too numerous to list. One purpose of all these is of course to offset whatever appeal Communism might have as an antidote to Thailand's already relatively painless brand of poverty. Taken as a whole, the program, which has been generally well-designed and well-administered, seems—contrary to the theories advanced by some recent writers on this subject—admirably suited to do precisely that.

U. S. aid to developing nations is, of course, by definition a long range affair. For example, Thailand's huge Yanhee Dam, which is now being constructed in the northwest, will be the biggest in Southeast Asia and will require six years for completion, but even this is not the whole of the time-span involved. Whereas such a power dam in the U. S. can be put to use at once, the same installation in Thailand involves educating not only its personnel in how to run it but also the entire national community in how to consume the product. This defect may be more apparent than real; the fight against Communism in Southeast Asia is likely to be a

45

long-range affair also, and Thailand is one of the few places where the free world has an opportunity, by planned effort over a substantial period, to show the superiority of its methods to those of the adversary.

A truer defect and also, fortunately, one more readily remedied may be that the program as a whole fails to attain maximum impact because so few people outside of the government officials directly concerned know anything much—let alone all—about it. The failure of the story of U. S. aid to reach the Thai public, and thus to produce as favorable a response as it should, is due to several causes, of which the most obvious and compelling is the propaganda provided by the opposition. Additionally, the aid program itself may have been to some degree at fault in failing to make itself intelligible to its chief beneficiaries despite such predictable obstacles. News about USOM projects, for example, has often been released piecemeal so that the essential feature of the program—its magnitude—is effectively concealed. Currently on foot are plans for publishing annually, both in Thai and English, illustrated reports of the whole program which should make it a matter of nationwide knowledge and permanent record, with corresponding consequences upon its public reception.

In its superficial effect upon Bangkok's cafe, and ECAFE, society, the Cold War, which is being as bitterly fought there as anywhere else in the world, makes scarcely a ripple. Secretaries from the Russian Embassy utilize the Sports Club as enthusiastically as their free world colleagues with the difference that, being proficient neither in pastimes that require childhood tutelage or adult leisure such as tennis or golf nor in the Southeast Asian *lingua franca,* English, they find themselves confined to more rudimentary forms of recreation, such as volley-ball and splashing in the swimming pool. On the margins of the pool, where the sunbath and sandwich area is divided up into national or linguistic groups, they occupy a niche of their own, shared sometimes by their almost equally isolated Czechoslovakian confreres. U.S.S.R. embassy parties, however, are attended by the Thai as well as the cosmopolitan community, with typical Thai absence of snobbery or prejudice.

That in the mid-twentieth century the warm, green, glittering capital of Thailand should provide, more than any other locale in the area, the background for a deceptively amiable mingling of two hostile worlds is, of course, much more than mere coincidence. It springs in fact from the nation's character and is a valid extension of the tradition by which that character was formed. To perceive why this should be the case requires a glance at Thailand's history, which is as strange and wonderful as anything else about this engaging kingdom.

4. Origins

As is appropriate for a nation with such a cosmopolitan destiny, the history of Thailand begins, circa 650 A.D., not in Thailand but elsewhere—specifically, in Yunnan, China. Already apparently imbued with the spirit of freedom and independence, Thai tribes, referred to in early Chinese chronicles as the "barbarians" beyond the Yangtze, had by that time organized themselves into the independent kingdom of Nanchao, whose armies fought numerous small wars with those of China. In consequence of these, the Chinese had overrun Nanchao and made it a tributary state by 1000 A.D. In 1253, Nanchao lost its independence entirely and became part of the Mongol

Empire of Kublai Khan whose renowned house guest, Marco Polo, may well have visited what is now Thailand on his way home from China in 1285.

Two or three centuries before this time, a few especially venturesome Thai tribes had begun emigrating from Nanchao into the hill country of what is now Northern Burma, Thailand and Laos, where the Shan, Thai, and Lao branches of the race respectively settled down. Shortly before the Mongol conquest of Nanchao, Thai armies overwhelmed the Cambodian garrison at the town of Sukhothai in North-central Thailand. Stimulated first by the Thai conquest of Sukhothai and then by the Mongol conquest of Nanchao, the infiltration from the North became a mass migration into what soon developed as a new Thai nation with its capital at the former.

During what is termed the Sukhothai era, which lasted roughly from A.D. 1260 to 1350, expert Chinese potters were imported to work in the celebrated kilns of Sawankhalok, whence their produce went as far afield as Borneo—though by what route or in what carriers are matters upon which contemporary archeologists often have sharp differences. Thais also came into contact with the already ancient civilization of India by trade routes inaccessible to the Chinese north of the Himalayan barrier, with notable consequences for their cuisine, calligraphy, and complexions. It was during the Sukhothai period that Siam became a nation

49

with a culture and character specifically its own. In retaining possession of this character through the intervening centuries, Thailand differs not only from the other nations of Southeast Asia which lost part of theirs through colonization, but also from the derivative nations of the new world, including the U. S., which never had this kind of character to lose.

→•King Rama Kamheng, whose forty-year reign started around 1275, enjoys a unique position in Thai history as the cultural as well as the military forefather of his country. He borrowed from the Khmers in Cambodia the alphabet which the Thais still use and extended Sukhothai authority southward to the sea and down the Malay peninsula. Shortly afterward, the era of Thai history that takes its name from his capital ended when a new Thai hero, Rama Tibodi, Prince of Utong, by capturing the Khmer strongholds of Chanthaburi and Lopburi, established a more centrally and strategically sited government at Ayudhya, some forty miles up the Chao Phraya from what is now Bangkok. It was during the Ayudhya period, which lasted until the Burmese conquest of 1767, that Thailand had its first contacts with the West and, through the exercise of adroit diplomacy, began to enact the unique role in Asian history that it has played with increasing skill ever since.

Thailand's first European visitor after Marco Polo was Duarte Fernandez, an emmissary sent to Ayudhya by Alphonso de Albuquerque, Portuguese Viceroy of India, who had just added Malacca to Portugal's then extensive empire in the Far East which is now represented by a few remnants like Goa and Macao. Treaties permitting Portuguese to live and trade at Ayudhya were followed by Portuguese missionaries and mercenaries, who contributed tutelage in Christian methods of worship and warfare. Both were welcomed, as were the Spanish with whose representatives at Manila a treaty was signed in 1589. The Spanish were followed by envoys, traders or both from the Netherlands, England, and France, as these nations began to extend their influence into the Far East. Toward the end of the seventeenth century, Siam became, so far as Europe was concerned, the most consequential kingdom in Southeast Asia, if not in the whole Far East, under the leadership of King Narai whose treasurer and general factotum was not a Siamese at all but an astonishing Greek adventurer named Constantine Phaulkon.

The stage was set for the great period of Ayudhya under Narai and Phaulkon by the successful outcome of a series of wars with Burma. These started disastrously enough in 1568, when the Burmese besieged Ayudhya for a year, captured it, and dominated the country for the next fifteen years. Thailand's young Prince Naresuan, absent during the siege, rallied a force outside the capital with which he was able not only to eject the Burmese from Thailand but also, turning East, to capture much of what is now Cambodia. When the Burmese attacked again, this time with an army of 200,000, King Naresuan, now celebrated as Thailand's greatest military hero, won his most renowned victory; while his armies defeated the Burmese horde, he defeated the Burmese Crown Prince in single-handed combat on elephant back.

The foundation for the next stage of Siam's development was laid after this heroic exploit when, while giving the Burmese a taste of their own medicine in the form of invasion, King Naresuan acquired possession of Tenasserim and Tavoy in South Burma. This gave Siam the major port of Mergui, on the West coast of the peninsula, fronting on the busy trade of the Bay of Bengal. A route from Mergui along the Tenasserim River, by pass across the peninsula jungle-hills, and then by sea diagonally across the Gulf of Siam to Ayudhya enabled travellers from the West to reach the capital without a time-consuming voyage through the straits of Malacca. It implanted in Siam the idea of two-front contact with the outside world which still crops up from time to time in contemporary proposals to dig a canal across the Malay peninsula, at the Kra Isthmus.

Constantine Phaulkon, also referred to in contemporary records as Constantine or Constance Faulkon, Falcon or Phaukon, was indubitably one of the most extraordinary Europeans who ever took a major part

52

in activities in the Orient, and, by the same token, one of the least known. That no competent biographer has as yet attempted a full length life of Phaulkon in English is certainly not due to any flaw in either the magnitude or the dramatic style of his accomplishments. One cause for the omission may be that the known facts of his early life are so disproportionately few that it is difficult to establish the relationship between his character and his contribution to history. Another may be that such information as there is about Phaulkon is scattered from the Gulf of Siam to Long Island Sound, so that collecting it all would be a heroic undertaking for any researcher. Nonetheless, what is known about Phaulkon makes it plain that it would be worth while to know considerably more.

During the late seventeenth century, British commercial interests in the Far East were represented primarily by the East India Company and secondarily by enterprising individuals, engaged in assisting or exploiting the company, as best suited their convenience —the latter being known in the idiom of the time as "interlopers." In 1670, a young Englishman from Bristol named George White arrived in Bangkok and began functioning in the second category. Phaulkon, an even younger Greek who had gone as a cabin boy from Cephalonia, where he was raised, to England, where he stayed long enough to learn the language, turned up shortly afterward and became White's assistant. Together, they became influential members of the highly cosmopolitan business community in that lively capital where ships from Japan and China as well as Europe tied up at the wharves or anchored in the Menam Chao Phraya, and where King Narai's brilliant court was comparable in its splendor to that of the Chinese Emperor K'ang Hsi at Peking.

As to how Phaulkon, starting from the position of a subordinate trader, became first an advisor to the "Barcalong," a phonetic approximation of an appellation which would now be spelled Phra Klang, meaning Lord of the Treasury; later an advisor of the King himself; and eventually, in effect, the Prime Minister of Siam are points upon which positive information is somewhat scanty. According to Thai records of the period as preserved in the largely untranslated *Annals of Ayudhya,* he first brought himself to the King's notice in ingenious and dramatic fashion by the way in which he determined the weight of a massive bronze cannon which His Majesty had recently acquired. After the court authorities had confessed to being baffled by the problem of weighing the cannon, Phaulkon offered his services which were somewhat skeptically accepted. He had the cannon placed on a barge, marked the consequent waterline, and ordered the cannon removed. Coolies then carried baskets of bricks onto the barge until it sank to the same level whereupon Phaulkon, knowing the weight of each basket of bricks, readily calculated that of the cannon.

Worried lest an alliance between the powerful Dutch and Mohammedan traders attempt to take over his kingdom on the pattern of what had already occurred in Indonesia, King Narai turned to White and Phaulkon in the hope that they could persuade the East India Company to counter-balance this threat by making Ayudhya a major base of British operations. White and Phaulkon apparently did their best in this direction but without success, whereupon Phaulkon concluded, perhaps in response to promptings by French missionaries, that if he could not bring the English into the situation, it might be possible to interest their chief rivals. When White went home in 1681, Phaulkon took steps toward carrying out this plan. Three of these were to become a Siamese peer with the title of Luang Wichaiyen, to embrace Roman Catholicism, and to send a splendid delegation to Versailles, where Louis XIV was just then at the zenith of his reign.

Meanwhile, in Ayudhya, Phaulkon set about consolidating the domestic situation as best he could until his long range cultivation of the French could bear fruit at home. As one of the first moves in this program, he thought it prudent to oust the Mohammedan officials who functioned at Mergui as *Shahbander,* i.e., Port Authority. To replace them, he chose Samuel White, younger brother of George, who by that time

55

was already on the King of Siam's payroll, as a captain of a royal trading vessel sailing out of Mergui. The younger White, unlike his brother, had been an employee of the East India Company on his arrival in the Far East half a dozen years before but this implied no bonds of loyalty or affection between him and the company. On the contrary, White's mortal enemy was the head of the company's station at Madras, who later used a small portion of the profits of his own career in the Far East to present a few books to a newly-founded little college at New Haven, Connecticut, thus causing it to perpetuate his name which was Elihu Yale.

Phaulkon's mission to France, surpassing even his own expectations, promised eventually to result in the dispatch to Ayudhya of an embassy including warships, engineers, and fourteen hundred men. Pending their arrival, Phaulkon's ambition to make Siam, with the assistance of the French the master of the Orient, with himself as master of Siam, came astonishingly close to realization. He maintained two palaces, one at Ayudhya and one at the up-river resort of Louvo, now known as Lopburi. Petitioners approached him on all fours as they did the King, who, ill with dropsy, left the affairs of state more and more in the hands of his brilliant counselor. Phaulkon's wife was known to the European colony as Lady Phaulkon and to the Siamese by a phonetic approximation of her real name, Thao Thong Keep Ma, or Dame Golden Horseshoe. Phaul-

kon had an English secretary named Joseph Bashpool
and was reputed to spend fourteen thousand crowns a
year on wine alone—a sum all the more remarkable in
that the Siamese climate is too hot to make excessive
wine-bibbing pleasurable even for Europeans—not to
mention the Siamese who even nowadays prefer non-
alcoholic liquors. Compared to the great British adventurers in the Far East through three centuries, like
Raffles of Singapore, Sir James Brooke, the White
Rajah of Sarawak and Clive of India, Phaulkon ranks
as at least an equal; and for a time he was well placed
to surpass them.

How and why Phaulkon failed to do so is a story
ably related in more detail by both E. W. Hutchinson
in *Adventurers in Siam in the 17th Century* and by
Maurice Collis, onetime British resident in Mergui,
in *Siamese White*. In brief, his policy, while apparently
effective against the Dutch, gave rise to intense jealousy
among Siamese courtiers whose relationship with the
King he had usurped and who suspected him, or pre-
tended to suspect him, of conspiring with the French
to take over the Kingdom on his own account. Under
the leadership of a general named Phra Phetraja, a
revolution conducted with Oriental thoroughness eventually resulted in the destruction not only of Phaulkon
but also of the King who had promoted him. Removed
from his palace to prison for two weeks of torture,
Phaulkon was finally taken in chains through the city

to the forest outside it and there hacked to pieces. After his death, Dame Golden Horseshoe was made controller of the royal confectionary, in which capacity she popularized various Portuguese delicacies made with eggs which are still among the distinguishing features of the Thai cuisine.

Phaulkon's meteoric career sheds a bright, brief light on a decade in the history of Siam as a flash of lightening illuminates a dark landscape on a summer night. The records of the trading companies, the memoirs of the diplomats, the eye-witness accounts by missionaries, one of which describes his last trip through the city, past the windows of his own palace in manacles, bring the city almost as vividly to life as the London of his contemporary Samuel Pepys, who indeed gives a hearsay account of it in his diary. After Phaulkon's death, the curtains close again, not to be reopened until the middle of the eighteenth century. The new regime in Siam proceeded to get rid of the rest of the foreigners except for a few Portuguese and Dutch through whom for more than a century only sparse and fragmentary contacts were maintained with the West. Meanwhile, the great wars with Burma, which had continued indecisively through most of the seventeenth century, took a new turn in the eighteenth when the Burmese, under a young and ambitious King, resumed the initiative and once more besieged Ayudhya.

In what may be very loosely styled Burmese War II, the first siege of Ayudhya in 1760 terminated unsuccessfully. It was soon renewed, and in 1767 the Burmese finally took the city. This time the defeat was even more complete than the one which had preceded it almost exactly two centuries before. The city was first pillaged and then burned to the ground, along with all its records, chronicles and archives, which were so thoroughly demolished that no one now knows for certain even whether the King and his court were dispatched on the spot or taken to Burma as slaves, along with thousands of their subjects.

As in the case of the Burmese domination in 1568, the Thai response to catastrophe was to produce a captain capable of retrieving the disaster. This was the celebrated part-Chinese General Phya Tak, or Taksin, who, with some five hundred followers, escaped from Ayudhya to the Eastern shore of the Gulf. While the Burmese were recouping their previous losses on the Peninsula—including Mergui which, deprived of its connection with Siam, lost its importance as a trading center and is now a sleepy little coastal town— Taksin reorganized his forces and marched up the road that now leads through the residential suburb of Bangkapi to capture Bangkok. Within a decade of the actual fall of Ayudhya in 1767, Taksin had driven the Burmese out of the country, revived the government with the capital at Thonburi and himself as dictator,

59

and re-established Thai rule over all its former domains except Tennasserim and Tavoy.

Perhaps understandably, the exploits of Taksin were such as to help induce in him a megalomania so pronounced that he eventually came to regard himself as a Bodhisattva, or future Buddha, whose actions were the consequence of divine guidance. Reluctantly, in view of his noteworthy services to the state, Taksin's ministers, who failed to concur with this exalted estimate, had him disposed of by the approved red-bag and banana-leaf procedure in 1782. Certainly the last, and perhaps the only, reigning Thai monarch to experience this drastic rite, which was more frequently inflicted upon errant princes, he was succeeded by one of his ablest officers, General Chakkri, later known as Rama I, one of whose wives was a Taksin daughter. Rama I moved the capital across the river to Bangkok and founded the dynasty which has ruled Thailand ever since.

5. *Recent History*

In 1931 a musical comedy called *Of Thee I Sing* enjoyed a highly successful New York run. In it, the noted comedian Victor Moore impersonated a fictitious Vice President of the U. S. whose absurdities were such as to constitute an agreeable satire upon U. S. governmental foibles. However, had the central figure of this extravaganza been called not Alexander Throttlebottom but Abraham Lincoln, and had he been portrayed, perhaps by a British writer using the international medium of sound film, as a rustic clown whose sole claim to fame was his competence as a raconteur of backwoods anecdotes, the U. S. public might have responded much less favorably.

The circumstances surrounding the celebrated movie

The King and I, which scored a resounding world success with Yul Brynner in the title role, were, so far as
Thailand was concerned, analogous to the latter situation. Like its several predecessors—the stage version
of *The King and I,* the stage and screen versions of
Anna and the King of Siam, and the book of the same
title by Margaret Landon—this film had as its original
source an 1870 book of reminiscences entitled *A British
Governess at the Court of Siam* by Anna Leonowens,
the governess concerned, whose relatives later established a prosperous commercial firm in Bangkok which
still does business there as Leonowens & Co., Ltd. The
discrepancy between fact and fiction in the original
memoirs, in which the author perhaps permissibly por-
trays herself as a major figure on the scene, let alone in
its later derivatives, may be judged from the fact that
the voluminous state papers of the King concerned,
whose historical title was Rama IV and whose personal
name was Mongkut, refer to Anna only once, as an
appendix to a shopping list. The relevant portion of
this document addressed to William Adamson, Esq.,
Branch Manager of the Borneo Company Limited at
Singapore and composed in the King's own English in
or about 1862, reads as follows:

"There is necessity for cough lozenges moreover
than an only one bottle you have had sent me lately.
There are many here who required me for their good
remedy. Can you obtain half a dozen or 6 bottles

thereof and send up to me here on next opportunity of the steamer Chau Phya? It would be best if it be so, otherwise please secure to order for the same from England. I wish but those which are genuine.

"My faithful agent Mr. Tan Kim Ching has told me in his letter to me that you and your lady has introduced Ms. Leonowens to him with an application that she will be an English School mastress here under the salary of $150 per month and her residence shall be near of Protestant Missionary here. For this we were hesitating on the subject considering that our English School will be just established and may be very small so the required salary seemed to be higher than what we proposed although proper because everything here cheaper than there at Singapore, also we wish the School Mastress to be with us in this place or nearest vicinity hereof to save us from trouble of conveying such the lady to and fro almost every day also it is not pleasant to us if the School Mastress much morely endeavor to convert the scholars to Christianity than teaching language literature etc. etc. like American Missionaries here because our proposed expense is for knowledge of the important language and literature which will be useful for affairs of country not for the religion which is yet disbelieved by Siamese scholars in general sense.

"But now we have learnt that the said Lady agree to receive an only salary of $100 per month and accept to live in this palace or nearest place hereof, I am very glad to have her be our School Mastress if the said information be true. I can give her a brick house in nearest vicinity of this palace if she would decide to live with her husband or maidservant, and I will be glad if she would make written best arrangement with my faithful servant Mr. Tan Kim Ching before she would come up here.

"When the said Lady came here and on being the Mastress of our English school would do good and be so active as her scholars might become in facility of language literature quickly and the study of School might so increasing as I would see her labour heavier than what we expected, myself will reward her some time or add her salary in suitable portion."

As a nation especially responsive to all sorts of verbal humor, the Thais would doubtless enjoy nothing more than a satiric portrayal, by Hollywood or any other agency, of a fictitious Siamese monarch. However, in precise ratio to the high degree to which Thai taste in such matters has been developed, such theatrical treatment of a real King, whose stature in Thailand is certainly comparable to that of Abraham Lincoln in the U. S., with whom he conducted an interesting correspondence, seemed to them less appropriate. From the Thai point of view, the salient indelicacy in this case was that King Mongkut, portrayed in the film as a light-hearted sybarite, was in historical fact exactly the opposite, having for twenty-six years prior to his accession to the throne lived the austere life of a monk in a Bangkok monastery. In the monastery, King Mongkut devoted a part of this protracted period to acquiring a grasp of Western science, history, and languages, especially English, as evidenced by his letter about Anna and numerous other royal documents, and another part to the founding of a new religious sect even more rigorous in its discipline than that to which he already belonged. The reign that followed was celebrated not for riotous living and dalliance with the governess but rather for royal courtesies to such Westerners as Queen Victoria, to whom the King sent a fine collection of presents, and Sir John Bowring, whose treaty with Siam in 1855 set the precedent for reopening the nation to trade with the West that had been in abeyance since the time of Phaulkon.

King Mongkut's decision to hire an English governess to teach English and western deportment to the royal princes was, to be sure, in line with his policy of rapprochement with the West, but it was scarcely its major expression. That not only this policy but the whole austere reign of the most revered monarch in Thai history should be commemorated by, and indeed Thailand known to the rest of the world chiefly through, the perhaps wishful recollections of nonexistent high-jinks in the harem is certainly more surprising than the Thai response to the film. This was

65

that a Thai Commission, well aware of the international importance of goodwill to the U. S. on the part of the Thai public, reluctantly forbade its showing in local theatres, to the consternation of its rather less considerate producers.

King Mongkut's correspondence with Abraham Lincoln, as distinguished from his correspondence with his Singapore agent, concerned not a request for a Governess and cough drops but rather an offer of much more substantial assets. Having learned that the President had suddenly become involved in putting down a widespread insurrection, His Majesty, for whom dealing with unruly tribesfolk was an everyday affair, graciously offered not only advice such as he was well qualified to provide, but also the means of following it, in the form of some war-elephants. What would have happened if Lincoln had accepted King Mongkut's generous offer and if General Sherman, who would surely have got hold of the elephants, had then used them on his celebrated peregrinations in Georgia is a matter perhaps best left to conjecture. In actual fact, the gift was declined.

The true story of King Mongkut's reign, as revealed in some of his state papers in English or Siamese, was ably compiled a few years ago in an as yet unpublished manuscript by two of his grand-nephews in the persons of M. R. Kukrit and his brother M. R. Seni Pramoj, the latter a pre-World War II Minister to the U. S., leader of the World War II Thai resistance movement in the U. S., and postwar Prime Minister. Its most affecting chapter concerns King Mongkut's death, of a fever contracted when watching a total eclipse of the sun at Hwa Kaw, near the Malayan Border, on August 18, 1868, to which he had invited a large number of European and Asian dignitaries as his guests in the fully justified expectation that his scientific prediction as to the moment of its occurrence would be confirmed by the fact.

According to King Mongkut, Thai history prior to the fall of Ayudhya, when all existing records were burned by the Burmese, has the faults of being "rather obscure and fabulous." Subsequent records, however, are copious enough to provide a fairly accurate notion of accomplishments especially during the major reigns of Mongkut and his successors. Under Ramas I, II and III, the last being Mongkut's half-brother whose elevation to the throne was what had caused Mongkut to retire to the monastery with his books, wars with the Burmese had been successfully concluded, due in part to British conquest of the area. Meanwhile, relations with the West had been resumed, starting with Portugal and culminating in commercial treaties with Britain in 1826 and the U. S., with whom Siam became the first Asian nation to sign such an agreement, in 1833. The reasoning behind King Mongkut's foreign policy, which was also pursued by his successor, was well out-

lined in a letter from His Majesty to Phraya Suria-
wongse Vayavadhana, Siam's Ambassador to France,
in 1864:

". . . The British and the French can entertain no
other feelings for each other than mutual esteem as
fellow human beings, whereas the likes of us, who are
wild and savage, can only be regarded by them as
animals. . . . I think that now is the chance for Britain
to put into practice her policy of bringing Siam under
her protection, since Siam is being harassed by the
French on one side, with the British colony on the
other. . . . It is for us to decide what we are going to
do; whether to swim up river to make friends with the
crocodile or to swim out to sea and hang on to the
whale. . . . Supposing we were to discover a gold mine
in our country . . . enough to pay for the cost of a
hundred warships; even with this we would still be
unable to fight against them because we would have to
buy those very same warships and all the armaments
from their countries. . . . They can always stop the
sale of them when they feel that we are arming ourselves beyond our station. The only weapons that will
be of real use to us in the future will be our mouths
and our hearts, constituted so as to be full of sense and
wisdom for the better protection of ourselves."

King Mongkut was succeeded by his sixteen-year-
old son, Chulalongkorn, or Rama V, whose equally
remarkable reign, after starting somewhat inauspi-

ciously with the death of his first Queen in the drowning incident recounted earlier, lasted until 1910. On acceding to the throne, his first official act was the promulgation of a decree abolishing the necessity for prostration by commoners when appearing in the presence of the King, on the ground that it humiliated the commoner and induced arrogance in the monarch. One of his last, started in 1874 but not completed until 1905, was to abolish slavery. While both of these acts were true to the motivations of his enlightened reign, both, like King Mongkut's equally characteristic hiring of Anna, are liable to some misinterpretation by Westerners, especially those unfamiliar with the Thai environment. By the time Chulalongkorn abolished slavery it had already become largely vestigial, involving not forced labor so much as the right of a laborer to sell his own work, as it were, at wholesale; so far as that goes the attitude of Thai masters to their Thai servants remains far more parentally responsible than that of Western employers, who may pay higher wages but often display what the servants regard as a snobbish disdain towards their personal affairs. As to prostration, this has been diagnosed by psychiatrists as being less a painful obligation symbolizing self-abasement than the enjoyable indulgence of an impulse toward retrogression into childish posture and irresponsibility, triggered by the presence of an esteemed father-substitute. Whatever it derives from, partial

69

prostration, despite Chulalongkorn's gracious decree, is still often and cheerfully performed in Thailand—if not by commoners before the King at least, in modified form, by many country tenants before royal or other landlords and, for that matter, by many junior members of Thai royalty before senior ones and by well-behaved Thai children before their parents.

During the reign of Chulalongkorn, Thai Ambassadors were sent to most of the major countries of Europe, able foreign advisors were brought to Bangkok and, partly in consequence of difficulties which developed in the Leonowens school for princes, the system of sending them to England was instituted as a more effective means of achieving the same end. Concerned like his father with the choice of making friends with the crocodile or hanging on to the whale, he ceded to France his claim to Cambodia and part of Laos and turned over some further portions of what is now Burma to Britain, receiving in return as much assurance as possible that Siam would continue to be regarded by both powers as a useful buffer state between them.

Chulalongkorn was succeeded by his son, Vajiravudh (Rama VI), whose decision to send Thai troops to France in 1917 was perhaps the most spectacular act of a fifteen-year reign otherwise noteworthy for his patronage of literature and the arts, his launching of the Boy Scout movement, in which he took a lively interest, and his failure to produce an heir to the throne.

His youngest brother, Prajadhipok, the seventy-sixth
child and youngest son of King Chulalongkorn, who, as
Rama VII, succeeded him in 1925, was an amiable and
cosmopolitan young man who secured his niche in Thai
history by being on the throne in 1932 when Thailand
ceased to be an absolute monarchy and became a constitutional one as the result of a coup d'état which set
the pattern for, and produced the personages who have
determined, the nation's political development ever
since.

In order to understand the character of the 1932
coup, it is necessary to be aware of the political view-
points obtaining at that time both within the royal
family and among Thailand's young intellectuals. As to
the latter, Thai students abroad, especially the thirty
or so who were studying in France, had become imbued
with the notion that absolute monarchy was outmoded
and should be replaced in Thailand by a constitutional
regime—preferably one in which they themselves would
have the major roles. As to the former, the Anglophile
King Prajadhipok had become imbued with more or
less the same idea and was quite amenable to drafting
a constitution and putting it into effect, as soon as appropriate steps could be taken to ensure its legitimacy.
Strongly opposed to any delay whatsoever in carrying
out their plans, the young men who were studying at
the site of the first great revolution in European history, and not far from that of its most recent one, came

71

home resolved to take speedy action. In so doing, they were favored by the fact that King Prajadhipok found himself obliged, under pressure of the world depression, to eliminate some of the senior members of his armed and civil services and to reduce the pay of the remainder. By allying themselves with displaced and aggrieved officers, the young conspirators were able both to prepare a practicable plan and to put it into effect upon June 24th, 1932.

Major figures in the group who plotted the coup were two young men about whom, as Pibul Songgram and Pridi Panomyong, Thai history was later to have much more to say. Barely over thirty at the time, Pridi was the son of a well-to-do Chinese merchant who had married a Thai wife and, as is quite customary under such circumstances, brought up his other son, Louis, as a Chinese. While Louis studied in Chinese schools in Singapore, Pridi went to Thai schools in Bangkok before proceeding to Paris where he conducted his studies for a doctorate in such fashion that the Thai Minister marked him down as possibly the cleverest, and surely the most revolutionary, of all the Thai post-graduate scholars in France. This rating, in part at least, may have been somewhat unfair to Pibul, a contemporary member of the Siamese Students Association in Paris who, in his own field, had compiled an equally distinguished record. Son of a far from eminent government official, he had done well enough at Bangkok

72

Cadet School to be chosen for further training at Fontainebleau near Paris, where he had more than held his own against top-grade European competition.

When, on June 24th, the promoters of the coup, styling themselves "The People's Party," presented King Prajadhipok with an ultimatum, the King not only replied that he was all in favor of the plan, but did it so promptly that the signatories of the ultimatum felt somewhat belatedly moved to acknowledge his response in a letter of apology for the emphatic tone of their previous communication. With Pridi as its administrative leader, Pibul as its military brain and a somewhat older German-educated colonel named Phya Bahol as a sort of liaison between the two, the coup government then got off to a flying start, under Phya Manopakorn, a former Chief Judge of the Supreme Court as its first Prime Minister.

In the remaining years before the outbreak of World War II, while the other nations of Southeast Asia were still struggling to graduate from colonial status, Thailand started a difficult course in comparative democracy, analogous to that which some of her neighbors are undertaking only now, with remarkable poise and rapidity. First major development in the new government was a split between Phya Manopakorn and the three other major figures, who handed in their portfolios. This led to a sort of secondary or echo-type of cold-coup, led by Phya Bahol and Pibul, in which

73

Phya Manopakorn was ousted on the premise that he wanted to restore the absolute monarchy. In due course Pridi, exiled to Europe on suspicion of Communistic tendencies at the time of the cold-coup, returned to be investigated on the charge by a special Commission, whose findings exonerated him but made it clear that his political views were well to the left of those held by his coup-colleagues. Finally, in 1935, the last reminder of absolute monarchic rule was removed by the abdication of King Prajadhipok.

The manner of King Prajadhipok's abdication was characteristic of the response to the whole crisis on the part of this gentle, sagacious, and far from autocratic, ruler. While he himself had been in favor of abolition of the absolute monarchy, he had come to feel that both his training as the embodiment of the old regime and his special relationship with the members of the new government made it difficult for him to put his convictions into practice. Under these circumstances, he ventured the opinion that it would be wiser for him to retire and hand over the job of developing constitutional monarchy to someone who would be unhandicapped by training for, and experience of, absolute rule. Although entitled to name his own successor, His Majesty refrained even from doing this, contenting himself by pointing out that a young king, who would be as little bother as possible to the Government, might be the most judicious selection. A Council of Regency

74

chose the pre-adolescent offspring of the King's deceased younger half-brother, then still at primary school in Switzerland, who, as King Ananda Mahidol or Rama VIII, was to enjoy a brief and tragic reign soon after World War II.

While all this was going on, Thailand's first general election had been held in 1934. One result of this was the selection of an Assembly in which half the members were chosen by popular vote and the other half appointed in the name of the King, by the incumbent government. Another was to make it clear that the vast majority of Thailand's electorate—now sixty percent literate, but then at the most generous estimate much less so—had no idea at all of the meaning of the great events that had been taking place in Bangkok or even, for that matter, that they had taken place. So far as that goes, a poll taken as recently as 1957 indicated that most rural Thais retained a degree of political naivete which may help to explain more recent developments in the capital. While well aware of the King and deeply devoted to him, few of them even by that time could recall having heard of Pibul, who was then well into the third decade of his career as the nation's foremost political personage.

6. *Current Affairs*

For a country faced with the hazardous choice between making friends with the up-river crocodile or hanging on to the deep-sea whale, world wars present a particularly painful dilemma. The object, naturally, is to determine as soon as possible which side is going to win and then join it. This is much easier said than done. The onset of World War II put Siam into a precarious position of which the risks increased as it became clear that Japan was planning this time to enter the hostilities against the Allies and that Thailand itself might become a battleground. Pibul Songgram, who later moved up from Minister of Defense to Commander-in-Chief and Prime Minister, had, in the former capacity, as early as 1938, foreseen the possibility of an eventual Japanese move against Hong Kong and Malaya, the latter to be made through Thailand. Meanwhile, Thailand, like all the rest of Asia, had been stirred by Japan's industrial and military successes, dating back to the turn of the century.

One of Pibul's more earnest advisors came up with the notion that, since some of the inhabitants of Laos, the Shan states and South China used a version of the Thai language and had a Thai culture, they should somehow eventually be incorporated into a "greater Thailand." It was in response to such ideas that the name of the country was changed in 1939, but an even more practical consequence developed, when, in 1940 after the fall of France, Thailand took advantage of the situation to demand the return of the territory that had been ceded to French Indo-China by King Chulalongkorn. After sporadic fighting, the matter was submitted to arbitration in Tokyo whither a mission headed by the suave and redoubtable Prince Wan Wathiakorn went to plead the Siamese case against the Vichy Government's Minister there. Not too surprisingly, the Japanese judgment favored Thailand, which got back two Cambodian and two Laotian provinces. Neither alteration proved to be permanent; the territory in question was all handed back to France after the War and Thailand, which became Siam again between 1946 and 1949, may yet become so once more in the future.

77

On December 7th, 1941, the Japanese Ambassador called upon the Thai Minister of Foreign Affairs, Nai Direk Jayanama, in the absence of the Prime Minister who was just then on an inspection tour of the Northeast provinces, to request that before 2 a.m. on December 8th—about the time of the attack on Pearl Harbor—permission be granted for Japanese troops to move through Siam en route to Burma and Malaya. Taken aback by the timing of this demand—the Thais had rather anticipated getting it in January, when a month more of dry weather would have made the terrain more passable—the Thai ministers requested permission to consult Pibul, who was hurriedly called back to the capital. At a dramatic cabinet meeting, with the Japanese Ambassador and military staff waiting in an anteroom, Pridi spoke for a group who wanted to resist while another group counselled outright and complete collaboration. Pibul—whose impulse to resist the Japanese had been somewhat dampened by a message from the British at Singapore to the effect that no help would be forthcoming from that quarter—chose the middle course of granting the requested permission but refusing either the active collaboration or the complete alliance with the Axis powers which had also been suggested. In a national broadcast, the Prime Minister assumed full responsibility for this decision— taken, he said, to preserve Thailand's independence. Thus began the somewhat ambiguous Thai policy of superficial collaboration with the Japanese accompanied by underground assistance to the Western powers which enabled the nation to emerge from the hostilities in a stronger position vis-a-vis the rest of the world than it had had when they began.

Within Thailand, the policy, as it turned out, involved not merely right of passage for, but polite occupation by, the Japanese. Foreigners—except for nationals of Axis Powers and neutrals like the Swiss—were promptly interned while the Japanese appropriated the Royal Bangkok Sports Club and Lumpini Park for encampments and motor-pools. The Government watched the rapid unrolling of Japan's offensive in the Far East with at least mild satisfaction, since it indicated that, by entering into what was officially described as an offensive-defensive pact, Thailand had apparently placed a hedged bet on the winner. By the end of January—when the fall of Singapore, German victories in Egypt and Russia, and the emerging significance of Pearl Harbor, made an Axis victory look increasingly probable—Pibul deemed it prudent under Japanese pressure to enlarge his stake by declaring war on Britain and the U. S. As a token of sincerity, Thai armies started a campaign in the Shan states on the right flank of Japanese armies in Burma. Goodwill missions were exchanged with Japan, and Thailand was awarded the four northern provinces of Malaya. Prisoners of war from Singapore and elsewhere were imported by the Japanese to work on the "death railway" to Burma, later celebrated in the cinema *The Bridge on the River Kwai.*

Outside of Thailand, the reverse side of this national ambivalence was much more conspicuous. In Washington, where M. R. Seni Pramoj, the Thai Minister, refused to deliver the Thai declaration of war against the U. S. on the grounds that it had been obtained under duress, the U. S. chose to regard Thailand not as an enemy but as an occupied ally. Seni called for the establishment of a "Free Thai" movement within Thailand, with which American forces could later establish contact, while in England, similar arrangements were proposed by Lt. Col. H. S. H. Prince Supasawat Sawatdiwat, who had lived there for many years. In fact, a Free Thai movement had already been launched by Pridi who became the organizer of its domestic wing and sent an aide to the U. S. to establish contact with Seni. By 1944, when allied victories in North Africa, the Pacific and finally Normandy indicated that the tide of war was turning, Pridi was able to establish contact with headquarters of the Southeast Asia Command at Kandy, Ceylon. There arrangements were made for parachute drops of Free Thai from outside the country—mostly Thai students who had been caught overseas at the outbreak of the war—accompanied by American O.S.S. or British Force 136 agents who worked together to organize interior resistance and send back further information to Ceylon.

As the war went on, the influence of Japanese occupation, handled with commendable circumspection by General Nakamura, the Commander-in-Chief at Bangkok, had curious repercussions upon Thai behavior. Apparently abashed by Japanese criticisms of easy-going Thai habits in dress and deportment, the government tried to enforce regulations to the effect that Thais should cease to wear their comfortable and appropriate national costume and instead contend with the tropical heat by bundling themselves up in coats, neckties, hats and even gloves. Husbands would kiss the wives goodby on leaving for work in the morning. The wai would be replaced by a Japanese type of bow and visiting cards would be carried and exchanged on the slightest provocation, as is *de rigueur* in Tokyo. European ball-room and ballet dancing would be encouraged, along with a modernized version of the Thai classical style. To promulgate and extend this program would be the business of a new government agency called the National Institute of Culture.

Such regulations, along with an unpopular scheme to build a new capital at the Northeastern town of Petchabun, presently brought Pibul and his government into disfavor. By 1944, when it was clear that Japan was going to lose the war, the Prime Minister took advantage of a defeat in Parliament to resign—thus

81

clearing the way for a successor who could try to treat with the victors as an ally. With the Japanese still in occupation, Pridi was ruled out, but his less eminent follower and deputy leader of the clandestine Free Thai movement, Nai Khuang Aphaiwongse, seemed entirely suitable. Nai Khuang made it his business to welcome wholesale parachute drops of O.S.S. and Force 136 agents, along with the supplies necessary for setting up a strong interior force. By mid-summer of 1945, the stage was being set for a major uprising that was only prevented from occurring by V-J Day.

From the time of his uncle's abdication in 1932, H. M. King Ananda Mahidol, whose father died in 1929, had been living with his mother at Lausanne, Switzerland, where he attended day-school and later the University. Early in December, 1945, he returned to Thailand, accompanied by the Princess Mother and by his younger brother, Prince Phumibol, to occupy the throne as Rama VIII. By the time he arrived, Thailand was approaching the end of a period of postwar confusion during which first Nai Khuang, then Seni Premoj, and finally Pridi himself had headed the government, while Pibul, after being held in jail for trial as a war criminal, had been released. With peace treaties and the political situation reasonably well in hand, it appeared that Thailand was ready for a prosperous convalescence from the rigors of war which, in actual fact, had not involved anything much more destructive than a series of long-distance bombing raids. This prospect was rudely shattered when, shortly after 6 a.m. on the morning of June 9th, 1946, the young King, whose demeanor had rapidly endeared him to both the government and his people, was found dead in bed, with a bullet through his forehead. The question that arose was: who fired the shot?

It developed that, in the preceding days and weeks, his Majesty had rather suddenly developed an interest in recreational revolver shooting. A short time before his death he had been given a new gun for his collection by Alexander MacDonald, a former OSS agent who had stayed on to start and edit the English-language *Bangkok Post*. Apparently it was from this gun, found lying on his bed, that the bullet had been fired just before the body was discovered by the two pages on guard at his bedroom door, who said they had run into the room upon hearing the shot. The pages also agreed that the King, who had taken a purgative the night before, had wakened about half an hour earlier and paid a visit to the bathroom; after finding him already dead, they raised the alarm, upon which his mother and brother were the first to reach the room.

Suicide seemed to be ruled out on two counts. One was lack of any apparent motive or mood; the King had been in good spirits and planning to leave Thailand—to visit Washington and then return to Switzerland to resume his studies—on June 11th. Another and even more compelling one was the absence of powder burns of the type almost inevitable when a revolver barrel is self-applied purposefully to the forehead. What might have appeared to have happened was therefore a classic case of the kind of mishap relatively common among neophyte gun-fanciers: passing the time before breakfast by toying with his new playthings, of which several others were on his bedside table, the King might carelessly have failed to realize that this particular gun was loaded. From the nature of the powder burns and the position of the body on the bed, it appeared possible that he had perhaps raised the gun over his head to sight it; that it had started to slip out of his hands; and that, in a spasmodic reflex impulse to regain his grip on it before it fell on his head, he had inadvertently pulled the trigger. All this reasoning from circumstantial evidence, however, would hardly have provided a satisfactory solution even if the victim had been an ordinary young man. He was, in fact, not an ordinary young man, nor even an ordinary young king. He was a King of Siam; and the protocol surrounding such Kings, together with the motives for foul play that must exist in the case of all such dignitaries, combined to make the hypothesis of accident seem inadequate.

Rules for the treatment of a royal corpse in Siam are elaborate and strict. They prohibit moving it about except in accord with certain ceremonies and only certain personages may touch the body in preparing it for cremation. All this precluded the performance of an immediate post-morten such as might otherwise have been in order. But even more to the point than the protocol restrictions governing the situation were the political considerations involved. Pridi, it was recalled, had been heard to express a preference for a Republican form of government; as sole Regent after the death of the other Council Members, he had been responsible for selecting the palace household personnel. What if the pages were in league with Pridi in a plot to get rid of the King? And what if some of Pridi's other loyal henchmen had seen fit to commit regicide on his behalf, outdoing the courtiers of whom King Henry II asked, in reference to Thomas à Becket, "Will no one rid me of this troublesome monk?"

The first announcement of the King's death gave the impression that it was the result of an accident but intimated that further details would be made available presently. These, however, failed to appear and rumors accordingly circulated that there had been a murder or at least that some important information had been withheld. An investigating committee including three senior members of the royal family was formed to help the police solve the case. Their findings seemed to support the theory that there had been foul play of some sort—though of exactly what sort has never been ascertained or at least publicly revealed.

85

As a murder, or accident, mystery the case of the King's death—ably described in more detail in *Brief Authority,* by the then U. S. Ambassador Edwin F. Stanton and in Alexander MacDonald's *Bangkok Editor*—is certainly one that would tax the talents of Sherlock Holmes and Perry Mason at the peak of their combined powers. More significant than its criminological fascination, however, may have been its influence upon Thai history, which is still far from wholly expended. One of the strongest reasons for believing that some sort of guilt may attach to Pridi is that he seemed strangely lethargic in pursuing the case. Shortly after the tragedy he offered to resign his office on the ground that the new King Phumipol had not appointed him to it. The hurriedly reconstituted Regency Council persuaded him to stay, but he resigned again in August, this time on grounds of ill-health, and went on a world tour. Pridi was replaced by Luang Thamrong Nawasawat, under whom postwar corruption began to reach new and distasteful proportions. The following November, in the first major post-war coup, Luang Thamrong was ejected and replaced by Nai Khuang Aphaiwongse, Pridi's former adherent, under whom the government showed signs of really getting down to work on the case of the King's death. Ten days after this government was installed, Pridi left the country, assisted by the U. S. and British legations in a display of gratitude for his wartime services which, however, stopped short of providing him with political asylum. After a period of residence in Singapore, during which he urged his Free Thai supporters not to resist the new government, Pridi proceeded via Europe to Communist China where, at last reports, he was in contented residence.

One possibility advanced by outsiders in the case of the King's death was that the King's younger brother, now H. M. King Phumipol Aduldej, might have been in some accidental way involved and then have been protected so as to evade the insoluble dilemma for the Thai monarchy which would have resulted from such a situation. This possibility is ruled out *a priori* by the thoroughly established fact that he was in a totally different and distant wing of the palace when the shooting occurred. Called to the throne under the most difficult imaginable circumstances as Rama IX, he has since handled the job with commendable diligence and dignity. Along with his strikingly beautiful young queen and their four handsome offspring—who, in addition to the Thai classical dance, have studied modern ballet —he enjoys popularity bordering on adulation. Thailand's present king enjoys the distinction of being the only monarch in world history to have been born in the U. S.—where he made his appearance at Cambridge, Mass. on December 5th, 1927, while his father, Somdet Chao Fa Mahidol, of Songkhla, was taking an M.D. at Harvard. Owing to an eye-injury sustained in a 1947 auto accident, His Majesty usually wears dark glasses in outdoor daylight and, unlike most of his compatriots who rarely stop smiling, rarely smiles at all. Brought up in Europe, where "le jazz hot" is considered a valid art form, the King is a clarinet-player and composer of professional rank.

That the present Thai custom—whereby, under a constitutional monarchy, changes in government are effected not by election but by bloodless coup—should be instituted elsewhere is, of course, open to question, although, in view of the alternatives often resorted to elsewhere, it might seem to have much to recommend it. In any case, what is indubitable is that the system should be better understood by outsiders, who often regard it erroneously as an unruly breach of the rules of political chess whereby, in effect, one player impatiently knocks all the pieces on the floor. Actually, the Thai coup is more closely analogous to what happens in bridge when, toward the end of a hand, the declarer, aware from the previous play where all the cards must lie, puts down his remaining ones together instead of playing them out. In Thailand, as in most of Southeast Asia, not to mention South America, military dictatorship is a normal phase of national development; and politics, to paraphrase Clausewitz, is often essentially a continuation of revolution by other means. If the other means include coups as well as elections, the coup does not as a rule take place until it is so apparent to all concerned that a new alignment of power has occurred that there is no need for an explicit test. Far from involving gunplay, like the noisier coups of Latin America, the classical Thai coup is an abstraction of violence in which shooting, while it may sometimes occur, is regarded as a serious breach of conventional decorum. As good a way as any to reach an understanding of this point may be a brief consideration of the major coup that comes most readily to mind, i.e. the one whereby the Thai government incumbent as of the date of this commentary acquired its credentials.

Thailand's 1957 coup, in which Field Marshal Pibul Songgram (who in 1948 had contrived to resume his former firm hold on the office of Prime Minister) was perhaps permanently ousted, was essentially a test of power between Police General Phao Sriyanond, energetic head of the Thai Police Force, and Army Field-Marshal Sarit Thanarat, Commander-in-Chief of the Thai Army. The position of the police in Thailand has been traditionally powerful ever since an early treaty with France specified that the frontier with Indo-China should be demilitarized, thus making it advisable to turn the national police force into a sort of subsidiary army to act as a border patrol. Under Police General Phao, however, who was the Pibul protege responsible for pushing the King's death case to its somewhat unsatisfactory outcome in the execution of three minor personages in the putative plot, the police had far surpassed their traditional quota of strength. Claiming, and getting, a share of U. S. military aid, the force had acquired its own tanks, airplanes and helicopters, some of which were used legitimately and others reportedly for facilitating an opium racket that made the wildest mischief of U. S. bootleggers look tame by comparison. In this ingenious caper, the police themselves allegedly dealt in the production of illegal opium for export, confiscated it from themselves, paid themselves a reward for doing so, and then sold the opium on the black market at premium prices.

For several years during General Phao's post-war rise to eminence, the inevitable rivalry between the police and the army for ultimate ascendancy in fire-power had been kept under control by Pibul, as a sort of make-weight between Phao and Sarit. In the general elections of February, 1957, however, the flagrant irregularities of certain candidates appeared to be so wholeheartedly condoned by the police that an impression became current that Phao might have it in mind to go one step further and set himself up as a dictator. Under these conditions, aggravated when Phao was promoted from head of the police to Minister of the Interior, his enemies, of whom there were an abundance, apparently proposed to Sarit that if he wished to anticipate Phao by making some move on his own account, he would have ample political support.

When Sarit had assured himself that, in the maze of

90

Thai political parties, he had enough backing to enable him to form a government, it was made clear to Field Marshal Pibul that he would have to get rid of Phao or take the consequences. When, with the quixotic loyalty often discernible in Thai politics, Pibul professed his unwillingness to do the former, the coupmakers proceeded to take action. Driving in his special new Citroen toward the seashore resort of Bangsaen for a week-end, the Prime Minister turned on the radio to get some music. What he heard instead was the news that Marshal Sarit had taken over the government and that his regime was finished. The Field Marshal by-passed Bangsaen and proceeded to the gulf port of Chonburi whence he made his way, late at night, by small boat, on stormy seas, to a gulf port on the Cambodian coast. After sojourns in the Cambodian capital of Phnom Penh and then Tokyo, he proceeded to Berkeley, California where, at last reports, he was living modestly in happy retirement. General Phao proceeded in the opposite direction, to Switzerland, where he is rumored to have invested most of a substantial nest-egg amassed during his tenure of office.

Marshal Sarit installed a three-month interim government under Pote Sarosin, former Ambassador to the U. S., and then, leaving his protege General Thanom Kittikachorn to hold the fort as Prime Minister, went off to Washington to be treated for a liver ailment. At last reports, both the patient and the new government appeared to be doing reasonably well, as evidenced by a subsequent "coup" in which Field Marshal Sarit, on his return to Thailand in the autumn of 1958, ousted his own Prime Minister, assumed complete power in his own name, and placed the country under martial law, thus in effect reducing the Thai coup to a form of solitaire.

7. Government

Despite areas of scarcity, mismanagement or both, Southeast Asia is a salubrious part of the world where living for the human species is in many ways easier and more agreeable than in northern climes. Partly no doubt on this account, the inhabitants of this clement region, at a time when Europeans were still shivering in caves or mud-huts and bashing each other with stone-axes or mere sticks, had long since grown used to a civilized existence. Great palaces were reared; vast empires flourished and decayed. Ships, much like the junks that still crowd Hong Kong harbor, commuted seasonally by trade wind across the Bay of Bengal and the Persian Gulf, working their way up through the

Red Sea close to the Mediterranean. Excepting for brief flare-ups, like that of Greece under Pericles or Rome under the Caesars, it was not until the Renaissance that Europe began to reach cultural parity with the Far East and not until considerably later that she was in a position to pretend to any sort of superiority whatsoever.

The superiority which Europe eventually acquired, through the deleterious development of gunpowder and other infernal mechanisms, was not of a sort to be much admired. It was, however, sufficient to enable her to swagger into the Far East with a bullying air, demanding rights of various sorts and killing the residents right and left when these were not granted with suitable celerity. A few Eastern potentates, like the Manchu Emperor of China who, during the reign of Victoria, instructed his advisors to find out who she was, maintained a reasonable perspective on the changing scene but most, unfortunately, succumbed to the violence of the European barbarians, much as Rome did to that of the Goths. By the end of the nineteenth century, Southeast Asia was, geopolitically speaking, a mere appendage of Europe, in which the Dutch held the East Indies including the densely populated island of Java; the British, India, Burma and Malaya; the French, Indo-China; the Spanish, the Philippines; and the Portuguese, most of the remaining snippets. In the whole of the Far East, only Japan, China and Siam remained independent and, of these three, Siam, the only one in Southeast Asia, was perhaps the one upon which the West impinged least painfully of all.

Since World War II Southeast Asia and its environs, through a combination of their own resources, growing perception on the part of Europeans and the example of Japan, contrived to throw off European control, with the result that India, Pakistan, Ceylon, Burma, Malaya, Indonesia, Laos, Cambodia, Vietnam and the Philippine Republic are currently experimenting with different schemes of governing themselves. However, while Thailand naturally sympathizes with these nations, it can scarcely be expected to place itself in their category so far as experience in self-government is concerned. Thailand has been governing itself to the reasonable satisfaction of most of its inhabitants for the past thousand or so years. Its closest approach to a genuine revolution, like those in the throes of which its neighbors have recently been engaged, took place as related, not against foreigners but against its own king, comparatively painlessly, in 1932.

The prevalence in Thailand of the cold coup d'etat as a means of changing governments—there have been some twenty-six major and minor coups since 1932, less than half of which involved serious gunfire and casualties—dates back of course to this original one, whose satisfactory outcome established the pattern for the rest. However, while there may be some doubt as

95

to whether the coup would be altogether suitable as a substitute for elections in neighboring countries which may lack not only this precedent but also the restraining influence of Thai religion and temperament, the efficacy of Thai government procedures, which would perhaps be noteworthy anywhere, is especially so when judged by regional standards. A working knowledge of these procedures might well be useful to outsiders generally and to its neighbors in particular.

Next to its propensity for frequent change by coup, and by no means unconnected with it, the outstanding peculiarity of the Thai political system is the unchanging identity of the politicos who do the changing. From 1932 until 1957, these have been mainly members of the first coup group, often referred to as the "Promoters," who, according to report, took an oath of mutual loyalty which may well be another factor tending to inhibit violence in their dealings with each other. If not members of the coup group, Thai cabinet members are normally at least members of the armed forces rather than parliamentarians; consequent sophistication in the rules of strategy and tactics may also be a factor in their customary readiness to acknowledge the outcome of rivalries for power in advance of an actual test of strength. A serious defect in the present Thai political system is its prospective lack of durability; when the promoters, now mostly in their sixties, die off or retire, no younger apprentice politicos adequately

trained in their duties, let alone bound by the promoters' curious code of behavior toward each other,
stand ready to replace them. Coups, of course, are not
provided for in Thai constitutions, though new constitutions follow coups so regularly that there have
been no fewer than six since 1932, with a new one
presently in preparation.

In evolving from the world's most theoretically
absolute monarchy to its numerically most constitutional one, Thailand has naturally proceeded with due
regard for Thai tradition. The latest constitutions tend
to season the 1932 original, largely composed by Pridi,
with that of 1949, largely composed by Phibul, along
with copious borrowings from earlier French, German,
and Anglo-Saxon sources. Thai Constitutions conventionally cover the whole scheme of Thai Government,
starting with the King, some of whose largely ceremonial prerogatives are modelled on those contem-
poraneously provided for the monarch in England and
some on the earlier provisions relating to this subject
instituted by King Boroma Trailokanath early in the
Ayudhya period. Such Trailok decrees as the penalty of
death for rocking the King's boat have been abolished
—perhaps somewhat superfluously since nowadays the
royal barges are in drydock most of the time and only
used for display purposes, like the 1957 celebration of
the 2500th year of the Buddhist Era. Others, like the
law of diminishing nobility, remain fully operative.

97

Among the King's ceremonial privileges are those of having a nine-tiered umbrella; no commoner may have more than one tier and ranks of nobility are graded somewhere in-between. The King is assisted in his duties by a Privy Council, an office of the Royal Household and an office of his Majesty's Secretary General. His administrative duties are confined to signing of legislation—upon which the signature of the Prime Minister is also required to provide validity—and, under certain circumstances, the exercise of a temporary veto. Nonetheless, the stability of the Crown, as a counter-balance to the coup, is what gives Thai institutions their essential quota of permanence and practicality.

Under Thailand's recent constitutions, the mainspring of government has been the Council of Ministers, i.e. cabinet, comprising from fourteen to twenty-eight ministers and deputy ministers chosen by the Prime Minister, who presides at its sittings. Council meetings take place twice a week; at them major policies are decided upon and major government actions undertaken. Cabinet members in Thailand have not, as a rule, been required to divest themselves of personal or commercial interests which may compete for, or coincide with, their official duties. On the contrary, the opportunity to invest in commercial enterprises, e.g. soft-drink distributorships, has normally been considered a legitimate perquisite of a ministership and during the early nineteen fifties so many high officials had franchises for so many different brands of bottled refreshments that political caucuses, at which each naturally favored his specialty, required as wide a selection as a well-stocked hotel bar. Through the ministries of which the cabinet members are the heads, the cabinet, in effect, runs the country. The National Assembly has been regarded as essentially a rubber-stamp legislature, though its debates may provide clues to the drift of influential public opinion.

Prior to the 1957 coup, an even better clue than the legislature to Thai political currents was often the so-called "Hyde Park," instituted by Prime Minister Pibul after his 1955 round-the-world-trip, which included a stop at London. On his return, the Prime Minister set aside the "Pramane Ground" near the royal palace, previously used mainly for royal cremations, kite-flying and Sunday promenades, as an area in which soap-box orators might give tongue after the manner of the lunatic fringe in London's celebrated outdoor forum or New York's Union Square. The difference was that both the United States and England have effective parliaments so that opinions voiced at such informal arenas need not be taken seriously. In Thailand, on the contrary, Hyde Park orators acquired a standing not fundamentally far inferior to that of Assembly members and their entirely free and

99

sometimes slanderous speeches were just as thoroughly covered by the press.

Thailand's legal system, modified by numerous subsequent events including the Burmese occupation of 1568 which had a lasting effect on Thai institutions, dates back to King Rama Tibodi I, who drew up the original legislative code in the latter half of the 14th century. His laws on Evidence, Offenses against the Government, and Abduction, while surviving more in the spirit than the letter of present day Thai ordinance, help to explain various Thai attitudes and social habits. Rama Tibodi's generous provisions regarding marriage are no longer literally in effect, but they set the tone for Thailand's relaxed and easy-going attitude toward connubial behavior. Early Thai kings, while possessed of absolute power, also had a close paternal relationship with their subjects. The great warrior-sage, King Rama Khamhang, for example, had a bell hung outside the palace gates at Sukhothai which could be rung by any citizen who had a grievance. When the bell rang, he emerged in person and handed down justice on the spot—just as King Abdul Aziz Ibn Saud of Saudi Arabia used to do in Riad as recently as 1945. Such royal obligations are currently reflected by the importance of *noblesse oblige* as a motive in Thai behavior.

For administrative purposes, Thailand is divided into seventy-one provinces, or *Changwats,* each with its governor appointed by the Ministry of the Interior, who represents the central government and co-ordinates the work of regional representatives of other ministries. He also presides over a provincial council of such representatives and of local civil servants, which corresponds on the local level to the Council of Ministers at Bangkok. Each Changwat is divided into *amphur* (districts), of which there are 411 in the whole country; each district into *tambon* (communes) of which there are 3,327; and each commune into *muban* (villages) of which there are some 50,000. Each district has its salaried (seventy-five dollars per month) district officer, or *Nai Amphur,* who is responsible to the Governor and who, with a staff of two or three assistants and three or four clerks, collects taxes, keeps community records, arbitrates boundary and other disputes, supervises elections and generally keeps an eye on all local developments. Each commune has a *kamnan* (chief headman) who, for a nominal salary of six dollars a month, measures lands, registers deeds, and presides over meetings of village headmen by whom he is selected subject to the approval of the Nai Amphur. Village headmen (*pu yai ban*) are elected by the residents, male and female, over eighteen if married and over twenty-one if not. The village headman, along with the Abbot of the village wat, is the major figure in most small Thai communities. Larger units than villages are governed by mayors who are appointed for towns and cities by the provincial governors.

Thailand's penal code, drafted by French and Belgian advisors and promulgated under King Chulalongkorn in 1908, lists nine types of felony and numerous misdemeanors. For the latter, penalties range from fines of five dollars to a month in prison; for the former more serious sentences are provided, up to and including death. In deference to Buddhist restrictions upon taking life, a somewhat elaborate subterfuge is resorted to in carrying out the latter on the very rare occasions when it becomes necessary. The condemned person is placed behind a target painted on a curtain at which a firing squad aims and fires. Thailand has no juries; cases are tried by one or more judges depending on the gravity of the charge. Each Changwat has a prison, with capacities of up to 2,000; juvenile delinquents go to work farms and training schools. Police outposts in the villages have comfortable and airy bamboo cages in which suspects are confined pending trial. The prison population of Thailand is about 20,000 and convictions for criminal offenses run to about 100,000 a year. Organized crime—outside the now greatly diminished trade in illegal opium—is relatively rare.

One reason for the rarity of crime in Thailand is the nature of its economy and the success with which it operates. Since most of the population is engaged

in agriculture, mainly rice-growing on small independent holdings, and since rice and other exports
produce a substantial revenue, economic pressures with
their attendant social strains are relatively mild. Thailand's fiscal policy, largely formulated by advisors imported from Britain (which still prints Thailand's
banknotes), has been strongly conservative, emphasiz-
ing balanced budgets and the importance of keeping
industrial imports down to a quota payable in rice,
rubber, tin and timber. Except for the brief period of
Japanese occupation, when it was linked to the yen,
the baht has been a remarkably stable unit of currency
which has provided evidence of the country's economic
strength even during some recent years of relatively
extravagant government spending. Thailand's main
economic problem is that of how best to achieve the
diversification and modernization for which the National Economic Council has prepared a five-year plan
and in which U. S. aid-programs are designed to be of
valuable assistance.

According to the Thai Ministry of Finance, which
still uses the personal crest of Constantine Phaulkon,
government revenue totals about two hundred and
fifty million dollars of which about one hundred and
fifty comes from taxes, chiefly import duties, almost
fifty more from rice export operations conducted by
the government, and the rest from other government
enterprises, fees, licences, fines and miscellaneous

sources. Personal and business income taxes are relatively lenient, partly because of the difficulty of persuading Chinese businessmen to divulge accurate and intelligible accounts. In government expenditures, which usually more or less equal income, the largest items are salaries and allowances for government officials. These, with defense, amount to about sixty percent of the total; the rest goes to various other expenses of government including about ten percent on capital investment in irrigation, transportation, and industry, and somewhat less than that on education. Thailand has a modest public debt, charges upon which normally amount to less than five percent of the total budget. Since most taxes are indirect, few Thai citizens are sufficiently aware of them to feel severely burdened thereby. Thai currency is fully backed by gold, foreign exchange or securities payable therein. The government manages the public debt and handles exchange control through the Bank of Thailand, which also operates a clearing house to which Thailand's two dozen or so commercial banks belong.

Since industry is a minor feature of the Thai economy, the labor movement in Thailand is relatively undeveloped and, since most Thais work their own land, unemployment is at a minimum. The non-farming labor force, mostly employed in tin mines, rubber plantations, and city service occupations, are almost fifty percent Chinese, except in a few occupations legally reserved for Thais, notably samlor-driving, which is practiced in Bangkok by thousands of young Thais from the impoverished Northeast. Labor regulations provide for a work-week of forty-eight hours, with fifty percent extra pay for overtime. Wages for unskilled workers, which may be as low as the baht equivalent of twenty five dollars a month, are likely to be supplemented by rations, housing and various sorts of bonuses and have a purchasing power in terms of needed goods of perhaps two or three times that much in the U. S. Office workers in Bangkok, e.g. stenographers who can speak and write English, get twenty-five to seventy-five dollars a week, depending on proficiency. Domestic servants get up to fifty dollars a month for No. 1 houseboys in European households, and down to five dollars a month for cooks' coolies.

Thailand's Central Labor Union, which was launched in 1947 with the support of Pridi, and which later joined the communist-dominated World Federation of Trade Unions, was later officially disbanded. It is reported to be still active underground and to have some 30,000 members, mainly Chinese in the ricemilling, stevedoring, and river transport industries. The Thai National Trade Union Congress, sponsored by Field Marshal Pibul a year or so later, was accepted for membership by the International Confederation of Free Trade Unions in 1950 and now has a membership of some 75,000 in some 75 industries. Thai labor organizations are not, as yet, a major force in Thai politics.

Public health and welfare in Thailand are major government activities under the Ministry of the Interior's Department of Public Welfare and the Ministry of Public Health. Health problems include serious diseases like leprosy, tuberculosis, and malaria, in regions where it still exists; urban sanitation, especially in Bangkok where many of the poor live in shacks or stationary houseboats moored or stranded in neglected klongs; and care for the aged or invalid, which has been traditionally a family responsibility. Traditional Thai therapeutics, especially those involving antiquated forms of mid-wifery and protection again mischievous *phi,* though still widely favored in the provinces, are being increasingly replaced by modern medicine as practiced either by missionary doctors or Thais who have studied abroad. Each of the seventy-one provinces now has a government health officer and at least one government hospital; in addition, each has an average of some ten rural health centers, the best of which are staffed by a qualified medical officer, public nurse, midwife, and sanitary inspector. Thailand has about two thousand modern doctors—one to twenty-eight thousand patients in the provinces and one to one thousand patients in Bangkok, which, partly because of its large European colony, also has ample and excellent hospital facilities, private as well as public. Thai dentists and surgeons are scarce but often unusually proficient.

Education in Thailand was, historically, the business of the Buddhist clergy, which ran the primary schools in the wats. Currently, schooling is compulsory for all children through the first four primary grades in government schools run by the Ministry of Education. Many of these schools are still on wat premises, where children are exposed to religious influence at an early and impressionable age. The chief weakness of the Thai school system lies in the scarcity of schools, especially secondary schools, in the provinces, where many children live too far away to attend regularly and hence fail their examinations before completing their courses. Almost a million children are registered for the first or pre-school class, in which they learn the rudiments of reading, and about a quarter of that number in the fourth, or last compulsory, grade. By the time they leave primary school, Thai children are supposedly fully literate, competent in simple arithmetic and equipped with a smattering of geography, history, and civics.

Secondary education, divided into two three-year periods, is limited to those who have done well enough in the primary grades to qualify, who can afford the time, and who live, or can board, near enough to one of the 1,100 government secondary schools to attend it. Completion of all six years of secondary school is a pre-requisite for most civil service jobs; Thai students who wish to attend universities usually need a special two-year preparatory course after completing the standard school curriculum, of which English is a requisite part. In addition to the logistic difficulties in attending Thai Government schools, a substantial economic obstacle for many pupils is the purchase of text-books, which are not normally supplied by the institution. In lower grades, owing to the scarcity of texts, much of the teaching is by rote or memorization. Both these difficulties are to some extent countered by private schools of which Thailand has about 2,000, some run by individuals and some by Christian missions, some for general and some for vocational training. Among the best secondary schools in Thailand, rated according to their academic standards, are the mission schools, of which the most renowned are Watana Academy, Bangkok Christian College, Mater Dei and Assumption College in Bangkok and Prince Royal College in Chiengmai.

Chinese schools, now only legal at the primary level, have dwindled from nearly five hundred to less than two hundred, half of them in Bangkok, at which some 25,000 students are enrolled. Teachers in the Chinese schools must be literate in Thai and use Thai as a language of instruction. For foreigners in Bangkok, there are numerous additional private school facilities. The biggest is an International School run chiefly for

U. S. children who, unlike those of most other foreign nationals, often stay in Bangkok with their parents throughout adolescence.

Thailand has five universities, all located in Bangkok, at which attendance totals some twenty thousand. Biggest of these is Thammasat, formerly called the University of Moral and Political Sciences, which—perhaps not without ulterior motives—was designed by Pridi to train public servants and which still functions largely for that purpose. Enrollment at Thammasat is listed at over 15,000, but since most of the students take correspondence courses and since many stay on the rolls from year to year without reference to their progress, these figures may be somewhat misleading. Oldest and best university in Thailand is undoubtedly Chulalongkorn, founded in 1917, which provides four-year courses in arts, education, commerce and accounting, science, engineering, architecture, political science, and public administration. Universities of Agriculture (Kasetsart), Medical Science, and Fine Arts, complete the roster. All Thai universities are handicapped by shortages of faculty and text-books; few good college-level texts exist in Thai and texts in English are prohibitively expensive. Thai university budgets tend to place more accent on architectural embellishment than academic content; Chulalongkorn's handsome Central Library—which contains some 40,000 volumes—cost more than a million dollars but its annual allowance for new purchases is less than five thousand. To acquire an education of Western academic standard, Thai students still have to complete their schooling in Europe or the U. S., where a total of about two thousand are usually in residence.

Thailand's educational system, public welfare and health, finance and economy, crime rates, legal procedures, administrative divisions and its political peculiarities are indubitably important subjects for specialized study and may also be of general interest insofar as they provide a yardstick for comparison between Thailand and other countries in the Far East or elsewhere. These aspects of the country, however—which are ably and more extensively examined in the *Human Relations Area File's Handbook on Thailand* in its *Country Survey Series*—are perhaps of value primarily because they represent that which Thailand has in common with the rest of the world. For an understanding of those more permanent and less ubiquitous attributes which distinguish Thailand from its terrestrial peers, and thus account for its primary significance thereto, it may be more appropriate to consider its diversions, its arts, and, perhaps most notably of all, its highly specialized religion.

8. *Religion*

So far as can be determined from the sparse and ambiguous records on this subject, Buddhism came to what is now Thailand, from India and Ceylon, somewhere near the beginning of the Christian era. Tradition places this event as early as the third century B.C.; the earliest tangible evidences of Buddhism that have been found in quantity in Thailand date from the sixth century A.D. In the 8th Century A.D. residents of the Chiengmai area were being converted in large numbers, through the efforts of a missionary Mon Princess named Cham Tewi.

In India, at and after the time of King Asoka, who reigned in the third century B.C., there developed a schism in Buddhism comparable in its dimensions to that between Orthodox and Roman Catholicism which developed in Christianity some centuries later. Mahayana, or Great Vehicle, Buddhism ("maha" meaning "great," as in "Maharajah," which is etymologically related to the Latin root "mag") projected the doctrines originally developed by the Lord Buddha into more complex philosophical and theological patterns of which the ultimate refinement is no doubt modern Zen Buddhism as practiced in Japan. Buddhism in its original form became known as Theravada (Doctrine of the Elders) or, much less respectfully, Hinayana (Small Vehicle), Buddhism, to distinguish it from its more elaborate derivative. In countries surrounding India, the two doctrines competed for acceptance throughout several centuries, with Mahayana gaining ascendency largely in the North, including China, whence it reached Japan, and Theravada gaining ascendancy largely in the South, especially Ceylon, whence it reached Thailand. From the 13th century A.D., Thai Buddhism has been essentially Theravada with some overtones not only of Mahayana but also of animism, astrology, and Hinduism involving gods like Siva and Vishnu.

Modern Thai Buddhism is noteworthy for the systematic way in which the Church, so to speak, is organized, contrasting sharply with the much looser arrangements obtaining in Burma and Ceylon, the two other major Theravada countries. The Thai Buddhist establishment is presided over by a Supreme Patriarch, or *Sangkarach,* chosen by the King from among nominees presented to him by the Ecclesiastical Council. This Council, whose members are chosen from the abbots of major wats, parallels the secular Council of Ministers, with dignitaries responsible for the departments of Ecclesiastical Administration, Education, Propagation, Public Works and so forth, under a presiding officer known as the *Sangkanayok,* i.e. clerical Prime Minister. The Ecclesiastical Council receives advice from a General Assembly which parallels the National Assembly. District or diocesan officials, comparable to secular government officials on equivalent levels, carry out the decisions of the Council in the provinces and districts. Church dignitaries do considerable travelling about on their diocesan errands; monks travel free on all Thai railroads.

When referred to individually, Thai monks are known as *Bikkhus;* collectively, they form the *Sangha,* or Brotherhood, of which the total membership averages about 150,000. Also resident in the wats are novices (*samanera*) and student-assistants (*dek wat*) who average about 85,000 and 120,000 respectively. Members of the Sangha must conform to certain regulations; they accept their food from the rest of the population, avoid handling money, wear yellow robes of a standard quality and cut, and own nothing else

except umbrellas against sun and rain, razors with
which to shave their heads and faces and a cloth
through which to strain drinking water or tea lest
they inadvertently infringe upon Buddhist principles
by swallowing a live bug, thus killing it. In addition to
the five moral precepts which all Buddhists are expected to wish to observe, and which prohibit killing,
lying, stealing, intoxicants, and adultery, there are five
more which apply especially to bikkhus: avoidance of
sexual indulgence of any kind; eating after mid-day;
dancing or singing; ornaments, perfumes, or luxurious
beds; and gold or silver. Monks also must abide by a
code of monastic discipline (*patimokha*) containing
some two hundred additional items.

Monks live in bare cells composing a dormitory
which is one of the main buildings in the conventional
wat compound; other architectural ingredients normally include an assembly-hall for the laity (*vihara*),
an ordination-hall for the monastic ceremonies (*bot*),
one or more *salas* (cf. French *salle*) or pavilions, one
or more chedis, and various facilities such as wells,
bath-houses and a library. Unlike Christian churches in
Protestant countries, which stand idle during most of
the week, wats hum from dawn to dusk with so much
diurnal activity that even the lively little churches of
Rome, where Romans gather to gossip, beg, and
squabble as well as pray to Heaven, would seem quiet
by comparison. Here villagers come—not to worship,

since there is nothing to worship—but rather to get advice from the monks, relay local news, rest, sleep, leave valuables for safekeeping, and attend to numerous other matters. Since half of the government primary schools are still located in wats, Thai small fry are likely to become personally acquainted with the local monks as soon as they are old enough to be self-propelled.

Seasonal variations in the membership of the sangha are due to the Thai convention, still obeyed by a substantial portion of the male population, whereby a young man spends anywhere from three days to several years as a monk, usually in his early manhood, often after the death of a parent. The most popular time for temporary membership in the order is the so-called Buddhist lent, i.e. the rainy season, between sowing and harvest. After ordination, novices may stay in the wat as long as they wish and may, or may not, become bikkhus. Novices wear yellow robes; temple-boys, who have no religious standing and merely help the monks with housekeeping and run errands, do not. Bikkhus may leave the order whenever they choose; only a small proportion stay in it for life. Wat routine for both samanera and bikkhus is comparatively comfortable but by no means relaxed. Shortly after dawn each morning, they walk through the village or town with their alms bowls to receive food which each of the villagers customarily has on hand to offer them. Back in the wat, they spend their time studying, reciting passages from holy writ or practising meditation. Lunch, the last meal of the day, must be eaten before noon. The afternoons are passed in further study, chants, and meditation.

For most non-monks, the practice of Buddhism consists largely of making merit, i.e. storing up credit to improve one's chances in a future life. Joining the order as a monk is the best way of making merit; those who have failed to do so are often penalized not only in their future existences but also in this one, by proportionate prestigial demotion. Other approved procedures for merit-making include building or helping to build wats; providing food for monks; and restoring to freedom animals or birds who may have lost it. Dealers in caged birds keep large numbers of them on sale in Thai population centers for purchasers who may wish to release them; on being released, more sophisticated birds may fly back to the dealers to be re-caged for the next merit-maker. Since anything done to benefit anyone, especially a bikkhu, is set down to the credit of the benefactor. Thai logic assumes that the benefactor should be grateful to the beneficiary rather than vice versa as is the custom in Christian countries despite the analogous precept that to give is more blessed than to receive. Householders thank the monk as they place their food in his bowl. The monk makes no reply.

Duties of bikkhus to the population—primarily to set a good example of behavior—also involve participation in the numerous ceremonies, mostly Hindu in origin since Buddha prescribed none, by which Thai life, especially family life in the villages, is accompanied. Most elaborate of such ceremonies are the rites and chants attending cremation—a procedure hygienically essential in a hot country with a high subterranean water-level. Others, centering at the wats, include rites for traditional religious holidays such as *Visaka Puja,* the anniversary of the date on which Buddha, by fortunate coincidence, was born, became enlightened and died. Buddhist wats follow a lunar calendar, differing sharply from the secular one. Observance by government offices or individuals of the Buddhist sabbath, or *Wan Pra,* contributes substantially to the slight uncertainty characteristic of Thai appointments all the more since the date of Wan Pra may differ according to the sect of the devout observer. The role of women in Buddhism is generally subordinate though a few become nuns, who wear white robes and perform social or religious services. The importance of the role of Buddhism in Thai life as a whole can be deduced from the fact that, whether or not he joins the Sangha, the average Thai invests from five to ten percent of his total cash income, not including food and volunteer labor, in contributions to his local wat.

117

The economics of Thai Buddhism and its administrative machinery are easy enough to describe. For the non-Buddhist, its intellectual and emotional content may offer less solid ground, starting with the question of whether Theravada Buddhism is in fact a religion at all. The answer to this would appear to be largely a matter of definition. If a religion is assumed to entail belief in a divinity of some sort, Buddhism is assuredly not one, for Buddha made no claim to divinity for himself or anyone else, regarding himself merely as a teacher and his doctrine as a prescription for existing as sensibly as possible. If, however, religion means a system of beliefs about the nature of life and the universe that satisfies the individual's need for a philosophy, a code of conduct and some ethical authority outside himself, then Buddhism is not only a religion but perhaps, from the viewpoint of some hypothetical objective observer, the best one that human beings have contrived so far.

Since religion in either case is a matter of belief, any description of what Buddhists believe by someone who is not a Buddhist must be largely meaningless; for without the content of conviction, the descriptive words can have no content whatsoever. However that may be, Buddhism starts off with the Four Noble Truths to the effect that life consists of suffering; suffering results from desire; cessation of desire results in the cessation of both suffering and re-birth; and this desirable outcome can be eventually attained by pursuit of the Eight-fold Path. The Eightfold Path consists of Right Understanding, Right Purpose, Right Speech, Right Action, Right Livelihood, Right Effort, Responsiveness to Truth, and Contemplation. Pursuit of the path leads logically to the five moral precepts mentioned earlier. Underlying all this are the Three Principles, to the effect that nothing is permanent, life consists of suffer-ing, and the soul is an illusion. The life of each indi-vidual, and for that matter the entire universe, is con-trolled by *Karma:* according to this, each action in each life calls for a certain reward or penalty either in this life or some subsequent one. After death, according to popular interpretation not always ac-cepted by Buddhist theologians, an individual may spend some time doing penance for bad acts, and some time being rewarded for good ones, in four possible major conditions, each with numerous subdivisions: heaven, life as a human, life as an animal, or hell. In rare cases, he (though not she: women must have at least one more existence, in male form) may reach the practically unattainable and totally indescribable state of *Nirvana,* which is the ultimate *desideratum* and ends the whole cycle, once and for all. Those inter-ested in a complete and accurate description of Bud-dhism can find it readily, and only, in the *Tripitaka* (Three Baskets), the Buddhist equivalent of the Bible, best read in Pali. Pali is the Buddhist *lingua franca,* wherein the Lord Buddha is supposed to have preached to his disciples who provided for its preservation so that the doctrine would remain fully intelligible to everyone regardless of national origins.

Foreign visitors to Thailand, most of whom are understandably quite unfamiliar with the Tripitaka, are naturally puzzled by many phases of Thai Buddhism. They wonder, for example, how Thai Buddhists can eat fish, not to mention meat, in view of the prohibition against destroying life. Rationalizations to the effect that, by taking it out of the water, the fisherman does not kill the fish but merely puts in a new element where it dies of its own accord, or that, if someone else has killed an animal, it does not much matter who then eats it, usually strike them as casuistical, to say the least. In fact, such rationalizations are perhaps justifiable on the grounds that when Buddhism, which started in an inland region, was brought to Siam, where fish provided the principal food for most of the population, the missionary monks solved the dilemma by applying the Buddha's teaching that if laymen cannot adopt the whole morality they had best at least be persuaded to adopt as much of it as possible. In any case, such dextrous compromises are at worst no more specious than numerous Christian ones whereby, for example, the competitive U. S. economy is considered to be totally compatible with the Golden Rule. What is more to the point is that Buddhism contributes substantially to a special, perhaps commendable and certainly refreshing, attitude toward many things, and especially toward property. To most Thais the notion that status or prestige should be accorded to an individual in ratio to his wealth would seem not merely unfortunate, as it may to many Christians, but, more simply, preposterous. This would represent Right Understanding; although, because of Right Speech, most Thais would be too polite to offend a purse-proud foreigner by saying so.

Another aspect of Thai Buddhism puzzling to many outsiders is the distinction between its two different sects, called *Mahanikaya* and *Thammayutika*. Here the difficulty may again be largely semantic; since it applies not to congregations but only to monks, the division is less comparable to that between Protestant sects, such as Baptists and Methodists, than to that between Catholic orders, such as Jesuits and Franciscans. The Thammayutika order was founded in the middle of the last century by the devout King Mongkut before he ascended his throne and may have derived in part from his close friendship with a Catholic missionary whose parish was not far from his wat and with whom he used often to discuss comparative religion during evening walks along the left bank of the Chao Phraya. It differs from the Mahanikaya—called the Great Sect because its member-monks outnumber the Thammayutika by about thirty-five to one—chiefly in providing for more strict observance of the *Dharma,* or religious discipline, from which its name derives. Thammayutika monks take more pains not to touch even paper money, maintain their wats in more austere style and pay more attention to the education and training of young monks than do their Mahanikaya colleagues. Owing to the regal position of the founder, their order also includes more members of Thai royalty and other influential personages. When H. M. Phumibol Aduldej joined the Sangha for three weeks in 1956, he naturally chose the Thammayutika Wat Bavornives, where the cell in which his great-grandfather passed twenty-six years is still carefully preserved.

Although, at the time of the 1932 coup, education of Thai children became legally the exclusive prerogative of the state rather than that of the Sangha, the state, through the Department of Religious Affairs in the Ministry of Education, still maintains close contact with the Sangha; religious instruction is mandatory in all Thai schools, whether or not the schools are located in wats. A major common enterprise in which the Government and the Sangha co-operate is the Monk's Hospital in Bangkok which purports not only to provide treatment for ailing monks but also to disseminate, through the Sangha to the nation as a whole and to rural areas in particular, modern concepts of public health and hygiene. Illnesses among bikkhus are numerous and, not infrequently, of psychosomatic origin.

Unlike the monks of Burma, who helped lead the campaign for independence from Britain, and of Ceylon, who constitute an important factor in current elections, the monks of Thailand have remained resolutely non-political. Theravada Buddhism, however, forms a strong bond between Thailand and three of its four nearest neighbors, Burma, Cambodia, and Laos.

One thing King Mongkut had in mind in founding his order was that the influence of abbots might well tend to decline with the inevitable, and otherwise desirable, spread of Western learning among their parishoners. While rapid sophistication by means of the press, radio and television has in recent years tended to impair their influence more drastically than even this foresighted monarch could well have anticipated, the Thammayutika Order has indeed taken judicious steps to preserve it. Of these, the most noteworthy has probably been the founding in Bangkok of a university, or more properly seminary, called, in honor of its founder, the Mahamakuta (Great Mongkut) University where promising young monks of both sects receive instruction not only in doctrinal subjects, as required by Buddhist tradition, but also in English and, when sufficiently proficient in it, such additional disciplines as Western Philosophy, History, and Comparative Religion. This effort to increase the erudition of the priesthood, now being undertaken also by the

Mahanikaya, at Mahachulalongkorn University, seems likely to ensure the continuation and perhaps even the extension of Thai Buddhism in a region that has by no means outgrown it.

Since, according to the most recent estimates, no fewer than ninety-four per cent of all Thais are practicing Buddhists, it might seem at first glance that minority religions were of small importance. Internal evidence would not support this thesis. In the first place, other religions such as Christianity are by no means incompatible with Buddhism, of which a salient feature is its emphasis upon general toleration. In the second place Buddhism itself has a Hindu foundation, perhaps analogous to the Hebrew foundation of Christianity, many features of which are still quite visible, not to say conspicuous. Finally, astrologers play a large part in the affairs of Thais: they not only fix dates and times for all important private or governmental ceremonies but are also prepared to offer predictions on all sorts of subjects, including winning numbers in the National Lottery. Thailand's astrologers belong to an Association which regulates professional practises and helps set fees which compare unfavorably with those charged by their perhaps less diligent colleagues in, for example, California. Twenty-five dollars is about average for individual horoscopes in which calculations as to the positions of planets and stars are based on the British Admiralty Almanac.

Religious toleration by the Thais is by no means confined to Christians; these are outnumbered, more than eight to one, by the nation's 670,000 Moslems, mostly Malayans resident near the Southern border, who, however, maintain as Islamic training center in Bangkok and number many respected converts among Southern Thais. Indian Hindus and Chinese Confucianists, Taoists, and Mahayana Buddhists also enjoy complete freedom to worship according to their diverse tenets. The Christian minority is composed of some 1,000 or so European missionary families and some 80,000 Thai, Chinese, or Vietnamese converts. Its prestige is commensurate with the value of its contributions to Thai education, medicine, and general adjustment to the modern world. The small minority of Thai Christians, like the Christian minority in many other Eastern countries, includes a disproportionate number of influential personages—some of whom may, of course, be Buddhists at the same time.

Christian missionary work in Thailand, which started with the arrival of the Portuguese early in the sixteenth century, has continued ever since without complete interruption even during the post-Phaulkon period. The Roman Catholic Church currently has over two hundred organized congregations and well over half of the total Christian community—which is the smallest in Asia in proportion to population. Major Catholic churches in Bangkok include Assumption

Cathedral; an American Redemptorist church built in the architectural style of a wat; and an ancient church near the river, noted for its midnight Christmas mass in which Thai-style angels attend the Nativity. Catholic educational enterprises include, in addition to those previously mentioned, a trade school for orphans run by Salesian fathers and a Jesuit student center in Bangkok, as well as smaller schools in Chiengmai, Hadjai, Nongkhai, and elsewhere. Among numerous Catholic establishments which concentrate on health and hygiene, the best known is Bangkok's St. Louis Hospital.

Protestant activities in Thailand did not get started until 1828 and only began to gain real momentum in 1832, with the arrival from the U. S. of the renowned Dr. Dan Bradley who, as an ordained minister, an M.D., and a practising journalist, was responsible for Siam's first printing press and newspaper, the English language Bangkok *Calendar* (of which the Oberlin College Library has the only extant file), as well as for its first surgery and first small-pox vaccine. Prior to his arrival, the only schools in Thailand were those in the wats. The Protestant educational establishment not only helped to generate royal interest in education, as evidenced by King Mongkut, but also resulted in a fine array of Christian schools currently attended by some 25,000 students in Trang, Nakhon Si Thammaret, Nakhon Pathom, Petburi, Pitsanuloke, Nan, Prae, Lampang, Chiengrai, and Chiengmai, as well as in Bangkok. There are major Protestant hospitals in half a dozen cities and, at Chiengmai, a leprosarium generally considered to be one of the best in Asia.

Among other noteworthy Christian efforts in Thailand which are directly supported by neither the Roman Catholic nor the older Protestant mission boards are numerous Seventh Day Adventist outposts and thriving YW- and YMCA's. Launching of the Thai YMCA in 1933 was due largely to the efforts of the father of the present king, Somdet Chao Fa Mahidol. One of its two establishments in Bangkok, the Boon Itt YMCA is named after a distinguished Thai Christian and YMCA worker who died of cholera in 1902. Boon Itt's characteristically cosmopolitan career included attendance at Williams College and Auburn Theological Seminary followed by seventeen years of residence at Watertown, N.Y., where he was a pew-holder in the First Presbyterian Church at which the presiding minister was the father of John Foster Dulles.

To attribute the compatibility between Buddhism and Christianity in Thailand solely to the accommodating nature of the former would be inaccurate. Christianity can also be a gracious faith and the U. S., while perhaps less officially hospitable than Thailand, has at least extended an informal welcome to Buddhists, allowing them to build wats in California and, more recently, even assisting them to do so in Washington, D. C. The affinity between the two faiths is perhaps also to some extent due to an essential similarity so marked that, far from its being difficult for a good Buddhist to become simultaneously a good Christian, it would, in respect to conduct if not to theology, be hard for him to avoid it. The similarity between the two systems goes far beyond mere doctrine. As engagingly argued by Professor K. C. Chakravarti in *The Indian Review* for January 1958, Christianity and Buddhism are closely related in ethical content, ceremonies, and myths, as well as in the organization of their respective monastic orders, whose similarities extend even to the detail of a specialized tonsure. Both faiths involve fastings, penances, lents, relics, haloes and religious edifices with pointed towers. Gautama Buddha and Jesus Christ both used parables in teaching markedly similar moral precepts—although there are no such parables to be found in the Old Testament and modern evidence suggests that the Buddhist *Jataka* tales reached Europe via Arabia, Syria and Greece, to become part of Western folklore. The births of both Buddha and Christ were preceded by divine annunciation to both mother and father; both children were produced in miraculous style. Wise men from the East, not West, came to Bethlehem, guided by a star; a star led Asita to Kapilavastu to pay homage to the future Buddha. Both Gautama and Jesus were concerned with miracles and each had disciples.

Fish in the streams of Quebec may differ in some

respects including size from those in the streams of New Zealand on the opposite side of the globe, but both types are often unmistakably trout. To the uninitiated this might seem to suggest either that trout were created separately in both places or that both environments were so similar as to produce almost identical evolutionary consequences. In fact, the answer to this piscine puzzle is far simpler. Trout were originally ocean fish which swam up rivers everywhere, including New Zealand and Canada, and then stayed in the fresh water. Ideas concerning the meaning of life and its presumptive aftermath are perhaps even more peripatetic than trout; they swim about in the oceans of mass-consciousness and leap in the currents of myth, working their way, often upstream, into all sorts of odd ponds and pockets. However, whether Buddhism and Christianity actually had a common source, or whether Christianity should properly be considered in one sense a derivative of Buddhism, are mere speculations; no one has yet found enough evidence to prove either thesis.

9. Arts

Because buildings are likely to differ more noticeably in purpose, materials and shape from place to place or time to time than most other forms of art, and also to be more durable and more conspicuous, architecture is the medium which often best identifies an area or an era. The eye-catching buildings of Thailand, which serve as a salient expression of and response to Thai character and environment, are a prime example of this rule.

Since Thailand is a country in which wind and cold are insignificant elemental factors but heat and rain important ones, the roof, which protects against the two latter, naturally has a proportionately more con-

130

sequential architectural role than it does in chilly Europe. More aesthetically responsive to this essential fact than some of their neighbors, the Thais long ago became specialists in roofing whether stationary or itinerant, like the King's nine-tiered umbrellas. In Thai buildings with any pretensions to architectural style, the roof is likely to be an even more conspicuous architectural feature than it is in the Chinese models from which they are no doubt derived. In addition to being highly functional, the roofs of Thai public buildings—usually extremely steep, to ensure both a quick run-off and ample insulation, built of bright glazed tiles, and often with ornamentally extended ridge-poles—are peculiar to Thailand and often startlingly handsome. The buildings which most advantageously display this structural specialty—like those which best represent the architectural idioms of Greece, Rome, and Europe but not of the U. S.—are usually religious ones. Of these the most celebrated— like Wats Po, Phra Keo and Suthat, whose roof-lines so pleased Somerset Maugham—are in Bangkok. As remarkable, though somewhat less special to Thailand than its temple roofs, are such other features of devotional *décor* as chedis and *naga* (serpent) balustrades. Since, for purposes of merit-making, construction of a new wat building counts for much more than the repair of an old one, most buildings in most wats are more or less dilapidated—which may add to, rather than detract from, their appeal.

Chiefly because of the technique of merit-making, Thai architecture, unlike that of many other countries, is excelled in durability by Thai sculpture, the best of which is in bronze, dating back to the fourteenth century. By this time, faint traces of Greek influence had reached Southeast Asia via Persia and India, as an aftermath of Alexander the Great's conquest of the former; the craft of casting bronze had probably developed separately and earlier, before the Thais left Nanchao. The most celebrated non-bronze statue in Thailand is its most famous religious monument, the Emerald Buddha in Wat Phra Keo, of which the ceremonial garments are customarily changed by the King three times a year, in accord with the season.

In Thailand, sculpture soon became almost entirely devotional and strictly stylized, being composed mainly of representations of Buddha in his four "suitable attitudes," i.e. walking, standing, seated, or reclining. Stylization of these images—which vary in size from the miniature to colossal reclining ones over a hundred feet long—derived from the fact that each portrait was a copy from another earlier and presumably more authentic one. Further insurance against variation was provided by the descriptions of Buddha recorded by his disciples. In line with these, his eyebrows had to be like drawn bows, his nose like a parrot's beak, his chin like a mango stone. However, inevitable variations or changes of fashion which crept in from one century to another—in such details as the shape of his top-knot or the length of the robe-lappet extending over his left shoulder—may sometimes serve to date the period of their composition.

Unlike Thai bronzes, the religious paintings even of much less remote periods are mostly in a state of even poorer preservation than the wats themselves, owing to the effect of the climate upon colors in tempera not chemically suited to endure it. Aside from the recently restored 19th century frescoes in Wat Phra Keo, the best preserved examples of Thai painting are murals in a half-dozen or so major Bangkok wats. Paintings on cloth or treated paper rarely date back more than a hundred and fifty years; most of them, like most of the murals, are vivacious treatments of scenes from the *Jataka Tales,* chiefly those concerning the exploits of Prince Vessantara, a dignitary whose role was that of the penultimate incarnation of the founder of Buddhism. A few, including those on the perimeter of the Wat Phra Keo, illustrate the *Ramakien,* as Thais call their version of the Ramayana, India's celebrated epic about the legendary King Rama (in whose honor the historic title of Thailand's present dynasty was adopted), his consort, Sita, and their insuperable monkey-warrior, Hanuman.

Contemporary Thai students interested in painting

or sculpture study these media at the University of Fine Arts under Acharya (Professor) Silpa Birasri (Auspicious Hero of the Arts), the latter being a representation, part transliteration of, and part complimentary pun on, his original name which was and is C. Feroci. Signor Feroci, who arrived in Siam from the Royal Academy of Florence in 1924 and who has been teaching and practicing art there ever since, is well represented in Bangkok by heroic bronzes like that of King Vajiravudh at the entrance to Lumpini Park. However, while these monuments indubitably embellish the urban scene, they are scarcely representative of the Thai classical style. While some of his pupils have displayed remarkable facility in contemporary painting, sculpture and interior *décor,* as exemplified by the lobbies in Bangkok's resplendent new Erawan Hotel, they may not yet have succeeded in blending traditional Southeast Asian technique with that of Western Europe as effectively as the painters of Japan have solved the analogous problem there.

Even more extensive than the influence of the *Ramakien* upon the content of Thai painting has been its influence upon the content of Thai music, especially Thai dance music, which is by all odds the most noteworthy. Apparently derived chiefly from Indian sources, Thai music differs from it, as it does also from that of Europe, by employing a scale in which seven full tones separate the notes of its octave. Thai instruments,

134

normally grouped into a five or ten piece band (*Piphat*), consist of two major types, woodwind and percussive, the former represented by a single oboe-like pipe called the *Pi-nai,* which is made out of rose-wood and sounds rather like a bag-pipe. Percussives are subdivided into two major sections, melodic and rhythmic, of which the latter is again subdivided into drums, gongs, and cymbals and the former into flutes and xylophones, all naturally of a special Thai variety and made of special kinds of bamboo such as *Phai Bong* or *Phai Tong,* which sound rather like their last names. Thai musicians sit on the floor before their instruments. Music racks are normally unnecessary; Thai music can be written down in Western style with some variations, but prior to 1929, when H. R. H. Prince Damrong Rajanubhab suggested that this be done in order to preserve at least the major classics, it was usually recorded entirely in the memory of performers, most of whom still play largely by ear.

The intricacies of Thai music are simplicity itself compared to those of the Thai dance. Thai boys and girls who wish to comprehend the latter usually, however, allow correspondingly ample time by starting their studies as soon as they have finished primary school, in the special classical dance academy maintained by the Department of Fine Arts. Here, among the boys, the first step is to separate the goats, who will play the roles of demons or monkeys, from the sheep, who will play the parts of heroes, like King Rama, and his brother Lakshmana. Meanwhile a similar but more complex weeding out takes place among the girls, some of whom will be assigned to male parts and some to female ones. When all this has been attended to, pupils begin to practice the basic posture of the Thai dance—seated with head, shoulders, trunk and waist erect, and hands fully stretched out. From here they go on to preliminary gestures of swaying slightly while bending their fingers back and bowing, then to standing up and moving slowly about, and finally to acquiring the essentials of histrionic interpretation.

Some indication of the complexities of interpretation may be deduced from a short list of some of the manoeuvres used in a brief episode called the "Destruction of Nonthuk by Phra Narai" in the Thai version of the Ramakien composed by its protagonist's namesake, King Rama I. These start with *The salutation of the celestials,* proceed to items like *the stag walking in the forest, the bee caresses (the flower),* and *the wind sways the tops of the plantain leaves,* and wind up with *the fish plays in the ocean* and *Phra Narai hurls the discus.* Evolutions in the Thai dance must be executed in traditional style, though occasional innovations may be introduced with the knowledge and approval of the appropriate authorities on the subject. For example, *stag walking in the forest* used to be represented simply enough by spreading both hands and bringing the palms to the front. Nowadays good dancers, "stretching forefingers and middle fingers out, clench the others, stretch the arms down until they are level with the seats, and invert the hands so as to bring the palms below, raise the first and second fingers till they are level with the waist and move them from side to side and up and down, alternately."

In Thai dancing, as in Indian dancing from which it presumably derives, the smallest movements of the hands, head, eyes, fingers or torso have profound significance, and audiences are expected to understand them all just as thoroughly as U. S. audiences understand the words of a song. Indian dancers, of course, have their own slang and represent the stag walking in the forest by clenching their fingers in an entirely different way.

The most usual type of classical Thai dancing—performances of which take place frequently during the winter season at the Fine Arts Department's Silapakorn Theatre—is one in which the performers wear elaborate traditional masks and costumes (deep-green for Rama, gold for Lakshmana, white for Hanuman) called the *Khon*. Another even more ancient and recondite form of the same art, from which the Khon may have developed, is the *Nang*, or shadow play; this, according to Thailand's distinguished authority upon these and many other cultural matters, H. H. Prince Dhaninivat Kromamun Bidyalabh Bridhyakorn, reached Thailand from India, where it originated, via the Empire of Srivajaya in Sumatra, Java, and the Malay peninsula. In the Nang, the story is told by means of large and elaborate silhouettes cut out of buffalo, bear, or tiger hide which are paraded in time to music before a white screen in such a way that the patterns emerge thereon. Since the movements of the bearers of the silhouettes, who hold them stretched across two vertical sticks, eventually became stylized into a form of dance, it is assumed that they eventually discarded the silhouettes, substituting masques. The postures of Thai dancers along with the emphasis in Thai dance upon manual manipulations might, among other things, tend to substantiate this hypothesis.

Presumably derived from the classical Thai dance-drama are three popular off-shoots in which the major ingredients are separately emphasized. One is the *Ram-wong,* a modern participational rather than spectatorial form, in which a circle of men surrounds a circle of girls and the two then execute a sort of circumambulatory chase, in which the couples weave in and out of the circles, without manual or other contact, in time to strains that sound rather like a gentler Thai version of the *mambo* or the *cha-cha-cha*—which, indeed, they may be. Another is a non-masked but serious dramatic form called *Lakon* usually based upon material other than the Ramakien. The third, called *Likay,* is an even more popular dramatic medium consisting of non-masked farce-drama in which dancing is not a main feature. Faubion Bowers, a U. S. expert on the Southeast Asian theatre, in his *Theatre in the East* comments as follows: "Likay is in every sense of the word a people's entertainment, with no less than twenty theatre houses distributed all over the city of Bangkok. Every night from eight to midnight persons from all classes, ricksha coolies, white-collar workers, and even those among Bangkok society who are genuinely keen on theatre, pack these Likay houses. . . . No temple fair or national holiday is complete without a special Likay performance—often out in the open air—with the actors performing on temporarily erected stages of rickety, shaking boards, against flimsy painted backdrops. . . ."

Reliance upon tradition in Thai art is no less conspicuous in literature than in dance, the drama and the song. Major ornaments of Thai classical literature in addition to *Ramakien* and *Jataka* include *Phra Law,* a romantic tragedy along Romeo and Juliet lines, supposedly written, in a mixture of verse and poetic prose called *lilit,* by King Trailok; the *Mahachat Kham Thet,* a chronicle concerning the activities of the Lord Buddha in his penultimate career as Prince Vessantara, which is especially popular among monks as a source for sermon texts; and *Khun Chang Khun Phaen,* a triangle drama of a somewhat more earthy nature, as may be deduced from the story-line. Khun Chang and

139

Khun Phaen, playmates in their early days, grow up to become rivals for the love of beautiful Wan Thong. Faced with the choice between Khun Phaen, a poor but gallant warrior, expert in the magical arts, and Khun Chang, a well-to-do but bald and cowardly landowner, Wan Thong eventually marries the former. Difficulties ensue promptly. Khun Phaen is dispatched to put down an insurrection and is erroneously reported killed in action, whereupon Khun Chang renews his suit. When Khun Phaen gets home, he finds Wan Thong apparently about to marry Khun Chang. This so irritates Khun Phaen that he leaves the premises, thus obliging Wan Thong to accede to the importunities of Khun Chang. Further give-and-take develops among the three until Wan Thong—who continues to hanker after Khun Phaen despite the fact that Khun Chang has proved himself to be a perfectly acceptable husband —finally gets beheaded, as a penalty for indecision.

Among the Thai classics, *Khun Chang Khun Phaen* has been by far the most accessible to Western readers through the English version translated by H. H. Prince Prem Purachatra, another royal Thai editor and *litterateur,* and published in regular installments as a serial in his English language *Weekly Standard.* With editorial judgment as to his reader's capacity for absorption of this classic sharpened by a journalistic apprenticeship as film critic for his paper's eponym, the London *Evening Standard,* Prince Prem wisely limited

weekly installments to a paragraph or two apiece, with
the result that the serial ran for several years. Contemporary U. S. writers who, when describing love
scenes, often nowadays find themselves bogged down
in a rut of four-letter words might do well to ponder
the far less restricted fashion in which the eloquent
author of *Khun Chang Khun Phaen* handles this type
of material which recurs frequently in his lengthy narrative. A typical example which, as evidence of mete-
orological responsiveness to human dalliance, may compare favorably with the earth-shaking passages in *For
Whom the Bell Tolls,* is represented by the following
excerpt:

" 'If I deceive you now, may misfortune pursue me
forever! Come, my dearest one, let me fondle that
golden skin of yours!'

"He removed his vestures and let them hang from
the screen. Then he took the girl into his arms.

"The breeze shook the blossoms and the pollen
scattered over the fertile earth. The place was filled
with a cloying fragrance. Under the moon and the
stars, the fireflies set the trees aglow.

"After the ecstasy of passion was over, Kaew Kiriya
began to feel the pangs of remorse. Khun Phaen asked
her if she was unhappy. . . ."

To Western readers the decapitational denouement
of *Khun Chang Khun Phaen* may seem a bit what, in
the vernacular of the California story-conference, is

described as "down-beat." To a connoisseur of Thai classics the opposite effect obtains, as may be guessed from a glance at an even better example of Thai trends in story-messages, that of a well-known novella called *The Four Jolly Robbers,* which may also be susceptible to brief synopsis. In this one, four desperate criminals escape from jail and, to elude detection, take up residence disguised as monks, in a deserted monastery. Here they not only succeed in throwing pursuit off the trail but in due course receive so much homage and largesse from the nearby villagers that, after passing their days in being accorded veneration, they can afford to spend their nights in happy carousing. All goes well until one day a young newcomer from a nearby village chances by the wat and sees their wicked revels, at which he eavesdrops long enough to understand the whole sordid story. Saying nothing, he hurries back to the village and spreads the word that the monks are really disguised criminals. The villagers react in peculiarly, though not necessarily typically, Thai fashion; they decide the young man is mad and take him back to the monastery where the head-robber blows pepper into his nose as a cure for his condition. The story ends with the young man running away to his home village in despair, pointing up the pragmatic moral, according to Phya Manunet Banharn, in whose collection of *Siamese Tales Old and New,* translated by Reginald le May, the story appears, that "If you live among folk whose eyes are closed, you had better close yours as well."

Thai modern, as distinct from classic, writing is largely Western in pattern and practiced by a fairly representative cross section of society in which the most conspicuous element, next to royalty like Prince Prem or M. R. Kukrit, whose best known work in English is a Thai Buddhist adaptation of *The Little World of Don Camillo* called *Red Bamboo*, are the lady novelists. Best known among these is Dokmai Sodh ("Spring Flowers"), in private life the wife of Nai Sukich Nimmanhaeminda, Thailand's leading bibliophile and a widely respected cabinet member in two Thai governments since World War II. The trend of Thai postwar fiction was influenced by a 1940 problem novel called *Yellow Race, White Race,* by Prince Akat Damkoeng, which examines the predicament of a member of the Thai aristocracy upon returning to his native land after education abroad. The last renowned Thai classical author was the court poet Sunthorn Bhu, whose *Swasdi Raksa (Safeguarding One's Welfare)*, a mid-nineteenth century favorite, provided a prescription in colloquial verse for the achievement of prudence, progress, and peace of mind.

Of late years, Thailand like all the rest of the world has become increasingly responsive to mechanical devices for dramaturgy like radio, television, and, especially, the cinema. Thai cinema production as a whole—

comprising two dozen or so feature length films a year —is never likely to loom large in world markets, owing both to the language-export problem and the specialized nature of its subject matter. Some Thai producers, however, have tried, gallantly or otherwise, to thwart circumstance in this respect by manufacturing for export silent but explicit short films of a much more universal nature which have also been available for local private showings. Meanwhile, film imports of all nations, especially the U. S., enjoy great vogue in part because of a typically ingenious Thai system for overcoming the obstacle of foreign language dialogue. Instead of disfiguring the film with marginal subtitles, this system, known to American film distributors in Bangkok as "Adam-and-Eving," consists of eliminating the alien sound track entirely and substituting "live" Thai dialogue which is read through a loud-speaker by one or more Thai actors concealed near the projection booth or behind the screen. Since such readings require split-second timing, considerable histrionic skill, and, for a solo performance, almost superhuman endurance, expert Adam-and-Eve practitioners are much in demand and earn considerably more than Thailand's best-paid movie stars.

The wide spectrum of Thai art includes numerous specialized minor arts and crafts. Among these, a traditional item has long been Nielloware, a form of metal work in which an etched pattern on silver is filled in with a black alloy. Thai lacquer, with elaborate gold patterns upon a black base, which was once exported all over the Orient, can now best be seen in the form of numerous examples of bookcases in the National Museum. The ablest remaining practitioner of this splendid art, an experienced specialist named Nai Lum, now ekes out a living—so modest that he has no apprentice to carry on the profession when he retires—by keeping these and a few other remnants in Bangkok wats or palaces in a state of fair repair. By contrast, the ancient craft of silk-weaving, now done in part with Japanese yarns, was revived so profitably after the war that it is now a thriving export industry.

Finally, like the Japanese, the Thais lay considerable stress on the art of flower-arranging although they naturally go about it from a point of view entirely their own. In Japan, whose culture is notable for its ultra-refinement, the object in flower arrangement is, of course, to produce an effect as close to nature as possible, through compositions of asymmetrical harmony in form and color. In Thailand, whose culture goes to the opposite extreme of almost complete spontaneity, the object, on the contrary, is to attain a pinnacle of artificiality. Flowers in Thailand are of course far more profuse there than they are in Japan or almost anywhere else, and include everything from the ubiquitous pond-lotus, which clogs up navigation in the klongs, to the rarest of orchids, which grow wild

145

in the woods and which Thai gentlemen raise in their outdoor hot-houses. For purposes of decoration, the custom is to string them like beads, pull the petals apart and re-assemble them in the shape of other flowers, or even, in extreme instances, give them a nice coat of paint.

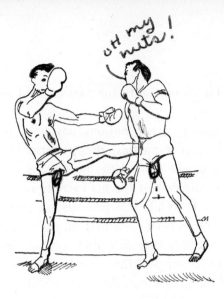

10. Pastimes

According to modern psychologists, games, pastimes, and diversions are to the nation somewhat as songs, hobbies, and dreams are to the individual. Insofar as they reflect the free play of subconscious preferences, they may be more indicative of character, if not of accomplishment, than the records of disciplined effort, which, in the authorized biography of the individual or history of the nation, receive greater emphasis. Intuitive precognition of this startling discovery may account for the fact that Plutarch, like contemporary profile writers, was a connoisseur of anecdote, and that Homer was scrupulous, in a justly celebrated passage, to record Greek partiality for parties, field games, and hot baths.

Rated against other nations past and present on their fondness for parties, the modern Thais would doubtless come in first, with the Greeks of Homer's time and all the rest of the field strung out far behind along the track. While it is perhaps not true of Thais, as has sometimes been said, that they play at work and work at play, it is true that they get fun out of both forms of endeavor and that this fun has in it a large element of the gregarious. As good an indication as any of the way in which Thais contrive to enjoy whatever they may be doing is presented to any passerby by the sight of a road-gang at work. More than half of the workers in such a gang are likely to be girls or young women whose costume consists of huge straw sun-helmets and dark pasins fastened by the heavy solid-gold belt which is at once a Thai working-woman's major investment and adornment. The work consists largely of carrying dirt or gravel about in shovel-shaped wicker baskets to the accompaniment of so much chuckling and joking that the passerby may jump to the surmise that very little is being accomplished. When it became necessary to repave a major Bangkok traffic artery a few years ago, a project which also involved channeling two major klongs into oversized sewer-pipes and then laying a concrete surface over them, many irate auto-commuters voiced irritable opinions that the job was taking too long. A foreign engineer was finally consulted on the matter and his opinion, handed down after earnest cogitation, was that, using American earth-moving machinery and the same budget, the work would have taken about fifty percent longer.

While Thais may to some extent make play out of whatever work they have in hand, it would not be fair to conclude that they regard games as a form of industry. A good clue to their real attitude in this respect may be the Thai response to, and influence upon, the game of golf. This form of recreation, first devised by dour Scottish shepherds to help them pass long days upon the chilly margins of their island fastness, had been conservatively institutionalized by the Royal and Ancient Golf Club of St. Andrews near Edinburgh long before the time that golf began to attract attention from the rest of the world. With docility comparable to that of its originators' herbivorii, the rest of the world proved content to play the game precisely as St. Andrews ruled was proper. Even rebellious Americans, who had been quite bold enough to win a revolution against England, did not dare do more to golf than add an altogether insignificant fraction of an inch to the diameter of the golf ball. It remained for the Thais to add a dramatically new element to the game.

According to the hallowed rules of golf as promulgated at St. Andrews, golf can be played by one, two, three or, at most and best, four persons. More than that number have no standing on the links and constitute a grave breach of the game's strict etiquette. The Thai innovation in golf consists simply of playing with eight, ten, twelve, fourteen or sixteen persons, and providing that numerically smaller matches have correspondingly inferior status. To the normal golfer it might seem that since a four-ball match moves twice as slowly as a two-ball match, a sixteen-ball one would remain practically stationary. Such a supposition would leave out Thai ingenuity as applied to all such matters. In a Thai sixteensome, the player whose ball is farthest from the hole on the green, putts out, proceeds to the tee and drives off without waiting for his partners. This turns the affair into a fairly steady procession, with a few players relatively stationary at the center and the rest making good progress ahead of and behind them. The consequent wiggling gait of the whole formation accounts for its slang designation, "crocodile."

The basic motivation for the crocodile is, of course, Thai conviviality; a Thai in the company of three other people inevitably feels practically alone and certainly would not choose to play any game under such austere conditions if there were any other way to do it. Golf in Thailand is especially popular among well-travelled sportsmen of whom many are political leaders, including three post-war Prime Ministers, their Excellencies Pote Sarasin, Pibul Songgram, and Seni Pramoj. Bangkok's two golf courses are laid out along and around race-tracks which, elevated above the surrounding terrain for firm footing, are necessarily bordered by klongs. To retrieve balls hit into klongs, Thai golf matches are conventionally accompanied not only by regular caddies but also by almost as many fore caddies as there are players. The spectacle of a crocodile moving majestically across the greensward of the Royal Dusit Golf Club, with its hordes of players and even greater hordes of caddies, would certainly surprise and perhaps strike terror into the Board of Governors of St. Andrews. Thai crocodiles often bear a closer logistic resemblance to military exercises than genuine Thai army maneuvers, or even coups d'état, since many of the participants are likely to be Army officers of at least field grade.

While the basic reason for the Thai fondness for golf may well be that, in its localized mutation, it provides such generous scope for the expression of the gregarious instinct, both before and after as well as during play, a contributory cause is doubtless the Thai love for gambling. However, while golf—in which Thai participants often win or lose the equivalent of a thousand dollars a round—offers a reasonably satisfying outlet for this proclivity, the major medium for this aspect of the sporting spirit is, of course, the national lottery. The national lottery, which was naturally one of the European amenities first imported to their native land by the earliest Thai travellers to that continent, pays off every five days, which helps to account for the fact that the few provincial newspapers that exist in Thailand are published at five- or ten-day, rather than weekly, intervals. Tickets are sold all over the country, largely by urchin hawkers, and the annual take has served not only to provide the Lottery Division of the Finance Ministry with handsome headquarters but also to render illegal all forms of private competition, including benefit bingo and the church raffle, which would otherwise no doubt have recommended themselves for revenue purposes to Thai wats with prudent and fun-loving abbots. As it is, the only connection that bhikkus have with the lottery is that on occasion, like the astrologers who handle the bulk of this business, they may sometimes, to oblige their parishioners, offer advice as to likely winning combinations. Such advice may or may not be the consequence of a period of meditation, during which self-hypnosis is so effective as to serve as an analgesic against pins inserted in the epidermis.

The lottery is gambling in its purest and most abstract form and golf is a Thai pastime only to the extent that it shows the national trait of cosmopolitanism as well as that of ingenuity as applied to sport. An instance in which gambling is integrated with a more truly indigenous Thai sport might be that of kite-flying, which also shows how a pastime which in most other countries is reserved for innocent children has been adroitly converted by the Thais into a thoroughly sophisticated device for adult gaming. Kite-flying in Thailand is, of course, extensively practiced by small fry, but they fly their kites less as a form of childish play than, like little-league baseballers, as a preparation for later life, when they may hope to become really expert practitioners. The season starts in March, when the monsoon from the East begins to blow, and Thai kite dealers display their wares at breezy spots on the perimeter of town—notably the entrance to Lumpini Park near Professor Feroci's imposing bronze statue of King Vajiravudh. Kites are flown all over Thailand but the major-league arena for this sport is the Pramane Ground, a handsome grass common bounded by the Grand Palace, Thammasat University, the Ministry of Justice and a major klong, which, as previously noted, is also utilized by Sunday strollers, "Hyde Park" orators, and the principals in royal cremations.

In Thai style kite fighting, the object is to not merely to get the kite into the air but rather to enable it to win an aerial dogfight against another kite. Battles between kites are patterned not upon mere modern air-warfare, which they vastly antedate, but rather upon the grander model of the battle of the sexes. In them, a star-shaped male kite, called a *chula,* attempts to fly in such a way as to cut, entangle or otherwise obstruct the activities of a smaller long-tailed female kite, called a *pakpao,* in such fashion that the latter falls to the ground. The pakpao tries to retaliate so that the opposite result will be obtained. Victory in such an encounter counts two points for a pakpao as against one for a chula which has an advantage in the weights. Big-league Thai kites of both genders, which may cost twenty-five dollars or more, are maneuvered by expert teams representing local business firms or other organizations, like U. S. teams of bowlers. A national committee schedules the major fights, which are watched by large crowds on Sunday afternoons, and awards prizes at the end of the season which reaches its height, so to speak, with the steady monsoon winds of February, March, and April.

In addition to fights between kites, Thais are partial to fights between humans, chickens, bulls, and fish. Thai cockfighting differs little from this specialty as practiced elsewhere all over the world, save that the game-fowl are closer to the original blood-lines of the breed, but Thai bull-fighting, practised mainly in the South, differs from the Iberian version of this sport perhaps even more dramatically than Thai golf does from Scottish. The most noteworthy feature of Thai bull-fighting, is that the *matador* is omitted, as are also the *picadores, muletas, banderillas,* swords and indeed all the other appurtenances of this sport so dear to the

154

European *aficionado,* while, on the other hand, instead of one bull, two are brought into the ring simultaneously and encouraged to devote their full attention to each other.

Far more evenly matched than bull-fights in the Spanish tradition, Thai bull-fights also last much longer, often a day or even more, by the end of which time both contestants are likely to be as gory and fatigued as John L. Sullivan and Jake Kilrain toward the close of their epic tussle in New Orleans as described by Vachel Lindsay.

In Thai fish-fighting, which is to bull-fighting as ping-pong is to tennis, two members of a resplendently ferocious species known to ichthyology as *Betta Splendens* are placed in a tank and encouraged to go for each other for the benefit of an intimate group of the fancy, most of whom wager heavily on the outcome. Betting on fish-fights is illegal, although the fights themselves are not.

Even more widely popular than cock-, fish-, bull-, and kite-fighting as a pretext for betting in Thailand is horse-racing, which in Bangkok takes place at least twice weekly, on the turf track of the Royal Sports Club on Saturday afternoons and that of the Royal Turf Club on Sundays, except during the rainy season when the former becomes too muddy to be useable. Horses are either Australian "griffins" (imports) or small tough native ponies, the latter usually running in fields which are numerically, and often in their shape, comparable to a sort of equine crocodile. Betting is done on the pari-mutuel system and the whole spectacle is often reminiscent of racing in the U. S. or Europe except for the absence of starting gates and, of course, effective saliva tests.

In a capital celebrated as the principal world source of illegal opium, the latter omission naturally has unpredictable consequences upon the form charts. It has been suggested that some of the Thai ponies would be more appropriately quartered in dens rather than stables, and indeed the aroma of Bangkok's best-patronized opium emporiums has sometimes suggested that this system may already be in use. When a horse who died of heart failure at the end of one recent race was found not to have been doped beforehand, it was suggested that the Thai S. P. C. A. investigate to see whether his demise was attributable to his having been meanly deprived of his customary pre-race stimulant. However all this may be, any shortcomings discernible in Thai racing are more than balanced by the convenience with which it can usually be watched from the comfortable and well-serviced veranda of a club that also probably provides more varieties of outdoor recreation, both per square-foot and absolutely, than any other comparable institution on the face of the globe.

Outside of auto-racing, perhaps the only major Thai pastimes, indigenous or adapted, for which the club makes no provision are those of *takraw,* basketball, and boxing. Thai boxing, as professionally conducted, is, like Thai golf, a distinctive blend of European and home-grown techniques. Before each bout each of the contestants executes a sort of combination of shadow-boxing, dancing, and prayer which represents at once a demonstration of technique and a ceremonial salute to his teacher and is considered also to provide some insurance against serious injury. Such insurance is clearly in order; the sanguinary fight that follows, in which kicking as well as punching is permitted after the manner of the more recently invented French *savate* or *jeu Marseillais,* and the fury of which is further enhanced by a ringside orchestra furnishing loud mood-music to accompany the action, more often than not ends in a bloody knockout. Most of the early evening programs at Bangkok's two pugilistic stadia, include three or four bouts each in Thai and Marquess of Queensbury style. Thai performers in the native vein who graduate to the latter are often of first-class ability, and several have been top contenders for world championships in the lighter classes.

The popularity of basketball in Thailand and elsewhere in the Far East, seems at first glance somewhat puzzling since this game, invented late in the last century by an American physical instructor to keep his charges busy indoors on winter afternoons, seems peculiarly ill-adapted both to the facilities and to the physiques of the inhabitants. While basketball can, if necessary, be played outdoors—as it must be in the torrid Orient which lacks gymnasiums—its more obvious regional drawback is that it puts a disproportionate premium on height. Thus the best players in the world would no doubt be African Dinkas or Shillucks, who live on the upper Nile, and often grow to seven feet or more, and people like Thais, Filipinos, and Japanese who average a foot and a half less, are at a grave disadvantage. All of the latter have nonetheless adopted it with an enthusiasm that almost makes up for their innate lack of structural aptitude. In Thailand basketball is nowadays played almost as universally and as enthusiastically as the indigenous *takraw,* which is a pastime perhaps better adapted for world export. In takraw a ring of players pass a small light hollow ball made out of woven cane among each other rather after the fashion of the pepper-games played by big-league baseball players in spring training camps. The difference is that in takraw the players are not allowed to touch the ball with their hands but keep it in the air by bouncing it off the head, feet or shoulders with thoroughly astonishing dexterity.

One of the respects in which Thais have not gone along with their British schoolmasters is in developing much enthusiasm for shooting or the chase. As might be expected in a devoutly Buddhist country, such pastimes are in the main left to more blood-thirsty Europeans who, however, can readily make arrangements for anything in this line that may strike their fancy. Bird-shooting may involve either snipe and plover in the marshes or dove, jungle fowl, and pheasants in the forests—the latter, of course, not a forced breed reared for execution but the original and indigenous version of this widely prized ornithological delicacy. Tiger-shoots may also be more readily organized in Thailand than in India, since they require neither cozy friendship with a Maharajah nor the expenditure of a small fortune on native bearers, *howdahs,* and high-powered rifles. About all that is required are stout boots, a good guide, and a steady hand on the trigger. The hills abound also in small Barking Deer which provide a noteworthy contribution to the Thai menu—although one which foreigners who have noted the unusually large quota of stray dogs allowed to meander about on the streets of most Thai towns, sometimes interpret as a gastronomic euphemism, like Long Pig.

Apropos of gastronomy, the undeniable fact is that, despite the Thai enthusiasm for all sorts of organized fun and games, their favorite pastime remains the basic one of nourishment. Old-fashioned Thais, when not eating anything else, are likely at least to be chewing on betel-nut, a gustatory staple as popular as chicle is in the U. S. and employed in much the same fashion—

159

except that betel-nut juice does not stick to the side-walk and the ingredients are carried about not in paper and tinfoil which defile the streets but in silver or wooden boxes which enhance the interiors of Thai drawing-rooms, as do the handsome floor-bowls required by the habit.

On chance meetings, Thais are inclined to repair at once to the nearest restaurant or sidewalk kitchen for an inbetween meals snack. The habit of frequent snacks and constant nibbling may be one reason that Thais are not especially partial to sit-down luncheons and dinners, as a form of social entertainment. The height of Thai gregarious enjoyment is reached not at stuffy banquets but rather at the outdoor fairs, informal, unceasing, and open to all, which take place at wats or elsewhere in all Thai villages annually at about Christmas-time with which they no doubt share a common derivation from earlier year-end festivals, such as the Roman Saturnalia.

Grandest of all such Thai carnivals is Bangkok's annual Constitution Fair in Lumpini Park, at which foreign countries contribute competing commercial exhibits, and which ties up the city's traffic for a week or more. Bangkok likes this fair so much that it is never quite dismantled; the children's train ceases to chug slowly around its miniature track through the park's lush greenery but the rails remain more or less in place and the merry-go-round spins and tinkles slowly through the whole summery year—as though to remind the citizens of that magic city, perhaps somewhat super-fluously, that the wheel never stops and that pleasure, no less than pain, no less than life, is never altogether at an end.

Bibliography

ANUMAN RAJADHON, PHYA. *The Life of the Farmer in Thailand,* translated by William J. Gedney. New Haven: Yale University Southeast Asia studies, 1955.

———. *Five Papers on Thai Custom* (Cornell University Southeast Asia Program Data Paper No. 28). Ithaca, 1958.

BENEDICT, RUTH. *Thai Culture and Behavior* (Cornell University Southeast Asia Program Data Paper No. 4). Ithaca, 1952.

BLANCHARD, WENDELL, ET AL.. *Thailand: Its People, Its Society, Its Culture* (Human Relations Area Files Country Survey Series). New Haven: HRAF Press, 1958.

BOWERS, FAUBION. *Theatre in the East: A Survey of Asian Dance and Drama.* New York: Nelson, 1956.

BOWRING, SIR JOHN. *The Kingdom and People of Siam, with a Narrative of the Mission to that Country in 1855,* 2 vols. London: J. W. Parker, 1857.

CHANDRUANG, KUMUT. *My Boyhood in Siam.* New York: John Day, 1938.

COLLIS, MAURICE. *Siamese White.* London: Faber & Faber, 1936.

COUGHLIN, RICHARD J. "The Chinese in Bangkok." *American Sociological Review,* vol. 20 (1955), pp. 311–316.

CROSBY, SIR JOSIAH. *Siam: The Crossroads.* London: Hollis and Carter, 1945.

DEYOUNG, JOHN E. *Village Life in Modern Thailand.* Berkeley and Los Angeles: University of California Press, 1955.

EMBREE, JOHN F. "Thailand—A Loosely Structured Social System." *American Anthropologist,* vol. 52 (1950), pp. 181–93.

GRAHAM, WALTER A. *Siam,* 2 vols. London: Alexander Moring, 1924.

GRISWOLD, A. B. "King Mongkut in Perspective." *Journal of the Siam Society,* vol. 44 (April 1957), pp. 1–41.

HALL, D. G. E. *A History of Southeast Asia.* New York: St. Martin's Press 1955.

HUTCHINSON, EDWARD W. *Adventurers in Siam in the Seventeenth Century.* London: Royal Asiatic Society, 1940.

INGRAM, JAMES C. *Economic Change in Thailand since 1850.* Stanford: Stanford University Press, 1955.

JANLEKHA, KAMOL ODD. *A Study of the Economy of a Rice Growing Village in Central Thailand.* Bangkok: Division of Agricultural Economics, Ministry of Agriculture, 1957.

JUMSAI, MANICH. *Compulsory Education in Thailand* (UNESCO Studies on Compulsory Education No. 8). Paris: UNESCO, 1951.

KING, JOHN K. *Southeast Asia in Perspective.* New York: Macmillan, 1956.

LANDON, KENNETH P. *Siam in Transition.* Chicago: University of Chicago Press, 1939.

———. *Southeast Asia: Crossroads of Religions.* Chicago: University of Chicago Press, 1947.

LEMAY, REGINALD. *An Asian Arcady: The Land and Peoples of Northern Siam.* Cambridge: Heffer, 1926.

———. translator. *Thai Tales Old and New.* London: Noel Douglas, 1930.

———. *A Concise History of Buddhist Art in Siam.* Cambridge: Cambridge University Press, 1938.

LEONOWENS, ANNA HARRIETTE. *The English Governess at the Siamese Court.* Boston: Fields, Osgood, 1870. Reprinted New York: Roy, 1954.

LEWIS, NORMAN. *A Single Pilgrim.* New York: Rinehart, 1954.

MACDONALD, ALEXANDER. *Bangkok Editor.* New York: Macmillan, 1949.

MASON, JOHN BROWN, AND H. CARROLL PARISH. *Thailand Bibliography*. Gainesville: University of Florida Libraries, 1958.

MAY, JACQUES MEYER. *Thailand* (prepared with the co-operation of the American Geographical Society). Garden City, N. Y.: Doubleday, 1957.

NATIONAL CULTURE INSTITUTE. *Thailand Culture Series* (pamplets), nos. 1–17. Bangkok, 1950–54.

NINTH PACIFIC SCIENCE CONGRESS. Publicity Committee. *Thailand Past and Present*. Bangkok, 1957.

PALLEGOIX, MGR. *Description du royaume Thai ou Siam,* 2 vols. Paris: Vialat, 1854.

PRAJUAB TIRABUTANA. *A Simple One: The Story of a Siamese Girlhood* (Cornell University Southeast Asia Program Data Paper No. 30.) Ithaca, 1958.

PRAMOJ, M. R. KUKRIT. *Red Bamboo*. Bangkok: 1955.

PREM CHAYA. *The Story of Khun Chang Khun Phaen,* Book 1. Bangkok: Chatra Press, 1955.

PURI, SWAMI SATYANANDA, AND CHAROEN SARAHIRAN. *The Ramakirti (Ramakien) or the Thai Version of the Ramayana.* Bangkok: Dharmashrama, Birla Oriental Series, 1949.

RANGTHONG, JAIVID, ED. *Souvenir of Siam*. Bangkok: Hatha Dhip, 1952.

REEVE, W. D. *Public Administration in Siam*. London and New York: Royal Institute of International Affairs, 1951.

SCHWEISGUTH, P. *Étude sur la littérature Siamoise*. Paris: Imprimerie Nationale, 1951.

SEIDENFADEN, ERIK. *The Thai Peoples,* Book 1. Bangkok: The Siam Society, 1958.

SHARP, LAURISTON, AND HAZEL HAUCK, KAMOL JANLEKHA, AND ROBERT TEXTOR. *Siamese Rice Village*. Bangkok: Cornell Research Center, 1953.

SIAM SOCIETY. *The Siam Society Fiftieth Anniversary Commemorative Publication: Selected Articles from the Siam Society Journal,* 2 vols. Bangkok, 1954.

SKINNER, G. WILLIAM. *Chinese Society in Thailand: An Analytical History*. Ithaca: Cornell University Press, 1957.
———. *Leadership and Power in the Chinese Community of Thailand* (Monographs of the Association for Asian Studies No. 3). Ithaca: Cornell University Press, 1958.

SMITH, MALCOLM. *A Physician at the Court of Siam*. London: Country Life, 1946.

STANTON, EDWIN F. *Brief Authority*. New York: Harper, 1956.

SUNTHORN BHU. *The Story of Phra Abhai Mani*, translated by Prem Chaya. Bangkok: Chatra Books, 1952.

THAILAND. Ministry of Agriculture. *Agriculture in Thailand*. Bangkok, 1957.

THOMPSON, VIRGINIA. *Thailand, the New Siam*. New York: Macmillan, 1941.

VELLA, WALTER F. *The Impact of the West on Government in Thailand* (University of California Publications in Political Science, vol. 4, no. 3). Berkeley and Los Angeles: University of California Press, 1955.
———. *Siam under Rama III, 1824–1851*. (Monographs of the Association for Asian Studies No. 4). Locust Valley, N. Y.: Augustin, 1957.

WALES, H. G. QUARITCH. *Siamese State Ceremonies: Their History and Function*. London: Bernard Quaritch, 1931.
———. *Ancient Siamese Government and Administration*. London: Bernard Quaritch, 1934.

WELLS, KENNETH E. *Thai Buddhism, its Rites and Activities*. Bangkok: The Bangkok Times Press, 1939.

WILSON, DAVID A. *"Thailand."* In *Government and Politics of Southeast Asia,* edited by George McT. Kahin. Ithaca: Cornell University Press, 1959.

WOOD, W. A. R. *A History of Siam,* rev. ed. Bangkok: Siam Barnakich Press, 1933.
———. *Land of Smiles*. Bangkok: Krungdeborragan Press, 1955.

YOUNG, ERNEST. *The Kingdom of the Yellow Robe*. Westminister: Archibald Constable, 1898.